Hell

Explained

Biblical Truth
OR
Orthodox Tradition?

HELL

EXPLAINED

BIBLICAL TRUTH
OR
ORTHODOX TRADITION?

DON KOSA

ACKNOWLEDGEMENTS

I cannot start this book without first giving thanks to the God and Father of our Lord Jesus Christ and His dear Son for their love and commitment to saving even the worst of sinners, and for pulling me out of the hell I was living in to see it all. Only by His guiding Spirit can I continue to grow in grace and truth, and enjoy the pleasure of expressing my gratitude forever.

I want to thank Bro. Harley Langley for his dedication to God, and his work producing the Holding Forth the Word publications for the Gospel Assembly and Christian Assembly churches. I will be forever thankful to God for every hand that contributed to the work therein that has so richly blessed so many. Countless souls honor the dedication of the ministry that has worked so hard contending for the faith that was once administered to the saints, and for pressing toward the mark for the prize of the high calling of God in Christ Jesus. May God continue to richly bless you all.

I want to thank my twin brother Ron, for helping God put me on the path of diligent study, and for being there when I needed him most. Equally faithful to me has been Bro. Rick Moore, pastor of the Green Gospel Assembly in Ohio. Thank you both for the years of dedication and direction, helping me to grow in Christ, and in the knowledge of the truth. Your leadership as pastors reached me in a "hands-on" ministry that many miles and years of separation could not hinder.

I want to thank my dear brother in the Lord, Bro. Paul Rainville, for helping me to get this work on the table. Thanks for every word and deed of encouragement, and for your eternal friendship. My gratitude for helping in this work goes out to Bro. Daniel Baer, pastor of the Mansfield Gospel Assembly Church in Ohio. Thank you both, and everyone else, that has believed in me in spite of all.

TABLE OF CONTENTS

A PERSONAL NOTE FROM THE AUTHOR

It has been my earnest desire to prepare and present to my fellow Christians a writing that could help them understand the truth concerning this subject. Months were spent in research through troublesome times. I consider them troublesome times simply because I realized that some things that I held to be true may not have been true at all. This was a very complex endeavor, which caused me to consider developing this study. Although heavily involved with many scriptures, easy enough to be understood by everyone; no matter how long they had been a Christian. It is hoped that it will be more easily understood by new believers since the tearing down of preconceived doctrines will not be necessary. So it has been my prayer during the preparation period, that whether the wineskins be new or old, the bottles would not burst. I ask any reader to be objective enough to be able to consider that what he believes may be dangerously wrong. Absolute devotion to the love of God and His dear Son, Jesus Christ, inspires, even requires, one to sincerely want to know the absolute truth in any matter, and desire to examine the accuracy of the things written herein. With those words in mind, I then ask you to stop before proceeding to the next page, and sincerely ask God to help you to understand each line of thought, as it is recorded for your spiritual health and growth.

Sincerely in Christ Jesus,

Don Kosa

INTRODUCTION

The Bible teaches us that hell has several definitions:

1. The grave, a place of silence, and the land of forgetfulness[1]
2. Individual punishment while still alive[2]
3. National punishment[3]
4. A state of being lost or in a false religion
5. Corrupt government and carnal worldly systems
6. The process of purification by God

I hold that hell is not the ever sizzling crackling place where Satan will stick people with a pitchfork throughout eternity. The true concept of hell is so simple that even a child can understand it. It has become difficult to understand because Satan has misdirected the minds of believers from the true Gospel on this subject through the development of false tradition. Satan is the deceiver! He will try to deceive even the "elect," if possible. We should expect this and be looking for it. An honest question that should be asked by all is "Is this a difficult doctrine, or has Satan sowed deception into the subject, thereby making the truth harder to see?"

Some religions believe that hell is simply the grave. This is not correct. In many scriptures it is simply referring to the grave, and in other scriptures it is not referring to the grave at all.

---

[1] Graves are pits.

[2] This is, simply put, being down in the pits.

[3] Similar to Sodom and Gomorrah.

Many understand that Satan uses truth to lure people to his lies. Many religions in this world display examples of this. On the other hand, sometimes truth, when contrary to ones beliefs, is mistakenly judged to be a lie. People throw the word "cult" around whenever they hear something strange coming to their ears. That's what many felt about Jesus when his words left them astonished. Please don't be guilty of that, as they were. Beliefs which might be deemed as cultish, and regarded by others as misguided, unorthodox, extremist, or false, might actually be true.

What if the most common teachings on hell were wrong? Wouldn't you like to know for sure what the truth is? Truth is what makes you free. Any teachings, other than that which is commonly considered orthodox, have been rejected throughout the ages simply because cults have accepted such teachings. It could be that Satan has deceived us if we reject any portion of those teachings, if they are in any way correct! Jesus' teachings contradicted established faith. By modern definition, Jesus' followers would have been considered a cult. Being considered a "cult" is not synonymous with blasphemy.

I feel that it would be fair to prepare the reader in advance for what he or she is about to read. I also feel that this exposition would be easier to understand if the reader knew at this point that I believe that the most common teachings on hell are incorrect.

God wants us to reason things through. *Come now, let us reason together...* (Isaiah 1:18). What is to be presented here can be rejected, or accepted; it can be swallowed, or it can be spit out.

I plead that you reason it through before passing judgment. If it does not hold water it will fall away, but if it measures up to the word of God, then it cannot be shaken. I am not asking the reader to swallow anything, but that you chew on what is presented here. Why should you consider this, or does it really matter?   By the time you've finished reading this, an understanding should be reached as to what the traditional views on this subject are, and why a <u>proper understanding</u> can be crucial to the salvation of many.

Some verses will be written out word for word from the King James Version, to allow the reader to follow along with ease. This is done to save the reader time. Defined words can be found either in Strong's Exhaustive Concordance or Webster's Dictionary Third College Edition. All underlining or bold face text within a quoted scripture is mine. There are many verses that are only referred to for scriptural verification of in-text points. The majority of these referenced verses may be known by the reader, perhaps even committed to memory. There will also be scripture verses that will appear as (see...). These will refer to verses which should <u>always</u> be read by the reader to get a better understanding of what is being revealed and discussed in this text. Scriptures will often be referred to more than one time. I therefore have assigned each verse with a designated number for quicker referral, i.e., (see # 1).

SWEET AND BITTER

Ezekiel was given a roll of a book, and told to eat the book. It was as honey for sweetness (Ezekiel 3:1-3). Something very similar happened to the apostle John as recorded in the book of Revelation:

1. **Revelation 10:8-10** *And the voice which I heard from heaven spake unto me again, and said, Go and take the little book which is open in the hand of the angel which standeth upon the sea and upon the earth. And I went unto the angel, and said unto him, Give me the little book. And he said unto me, Take it, and eat it up; and it shall make thy belly bitter, but it shall be in thy mouth sweet as honey. And I took the little book out of the angel's hand, and ate it up; and it was in my mouth sweet as honey: and as soon as I had eaten it, my belly was bitter.*

This signifies that he received the word of God by faith, which is often compared to honey.

2. **Psalms 119:103** *How sweet are thy words unto my taste! yea, sweeter than honey to my mouth!*

3. **Jeremiah 15:16** *Thy words were found, and I did eat them; and thy word was unto me the joy and rejoicing of mine heart: for I am called by thy name, O LORD God of hosts.*

The word of God is sweet to the soul because it brings joy and everlasting life, but is bitter in the belly because it is contrary to our carnal nature. Jesus is the Word of God (John 1:1). He likened himself to manna, as the true and living spiritual bread

15

from Heaven (John 6:22-33).[4]

> 4. **Exodus 16:31** *And the house of Israel called the name thereof Manna: and it was like coriander seed, white; and the taste of it was like wafers made with honey.*
>
> 5a. **John 1:14** *And the Word was made flesh, and dwelt among us, (and we beheld his glory, the glory as of the only begotten of the Father,) full of grace and truth.*
>
> 5b. **John 6:51** *I am the living bread which came down from heaven: if any man eat of this bread, he shall live for ever: and the bread that I will give is my flesh, which I will give for the life of the world.*
>
> 6a. **John 6:58** *This is that bread which came down from heaven: not as your fathers did eat manna, and are dead: he that eateth of this bread shall live for ever.*
>
> 6b. **John 6:48** *I am that bread of life.*
>
> 6c. **John 6:33** *For the bread of God is he which cometh down from heaven, and giveth life unto the world.*

That's sweet! There is no reason to spit it out. If you do, you will never be nourished by it, and you will starve to death spiritually. Jesus said that if we eat of (accept) Him, we will **live** forever. Just as Ezekiel and John received (ate) the words that were given to them, we receive (accept) Jesus, eating the

---

[4] Jesus=Word=Manna.

Bread of Life, the Word of God. So then if we accept Him, we will live forever. We will have everlasting life (John 3:16), will never see death (John 8:51), and will not be hurt of the second death (Revelation 2:11). Truth is the "sweetness" that Jesus described in John 17:17 when he said "Thy Word is truth."

If truth is contrary to what we <u>believe</u>, it will strike us as tasting bitter. If I learned that my beliefs were against the Word of God, I would be sick to my stomach, as if I had eaten something very bitter. This is what happened to the prophets.

TRADITION GETS THE BOOT

The Bible doesn't tell me that if I reject Christ I will live forever. In fact, it says the opposite. It uses terms like "perish," "death," and "destruction."

Whoops! There's the bitterness. Why is it bitter? Perhaps it is because that is not what we thought the whole tenor of the Bible taught. Now, one might believe that I am placing irreverent hands on the ark of the covenant, but if I am correct I should be able to prove it by using the word of God, not by twisting it as so many do, but by allowing it to be the final authority regarding my faith.

The first session of the Council of Trent (1545-47 A.D.) stated as one of its first decrees that the scripture had to be understood within the confines of the "tradition" of the church. This was an implicit rejection of the Protestant principle of *sola scriptura*.[5] This put limitations on what the Bible said, and opened a Pandora's box of doctrines that were "alongside" (or outside) of scripture.

Jesus often said *have ye not read...?* (Matthew 12:3, 19:4, 21:16, and 22:31). I also ask, as He did, that we "toss aside" tradition if it does not stand up to scripture, as I caution all "...do ye not hear the law?" In 1 Peter 1:18, Peter states: *Forasmuch as ye know that ye were not redeemed with corruptible things, as silver and gold, from your vain conversation received by tradition from your fathers....* In Mark 7:8-9 it speaks quite plainly of men's traditions: *For*

---

[5] Literally meaning "scripture alone."

laying aside the commandment of God, ye hold the tradition of men as the washing of pots and cups: and many other such like things ye do. And he said unto them, Full well ye reject the commandment of God that ye may keep your own tradition. In both of these verses the traditions being discussed are not secular, but the religious traditions of the Pharisees, which were held by them to be holy traditions (see Mark 1:3, 5, 13, and Matthew 15:2, 3, 6).

Now before you begin thinking that I am walking on unholy water, I must state that I realize there is a lot of explaining to do before anyone can begin to taste this hard to chew meat (see Hebrews 5:1-2). I will need to explain the Lake of Fire, torments night and day, the fire that is not quenched, the worm that dieth not, eternal punishment, and the Parable of Lazarus and the Rich Man.

Two particular doctrines found in Hebrews 6:2 must be examined to fully understand what will be presented here: eternal judgment and the resurrection of the dead.

SOUL SLEEP

First, allow me to clarify why many people do not believe in soul sleep. We know that the spirit that is in man came from God. God breathed into his nostrils the breath of life,[6] and it was only then that man became a living soul (Genesis 2:7), for it is the spirit that quickeneth (makes alive). The word "breath" denotes divine intellect; a part of God's Spirit. This is what "goeth upwards" at the death of man to return to where it came from (Ecclesiastes 3:21). The word for spirit in Hebrew is *ruach*, which can mean spirit, breath, perception, or smell. Just as a person senses good and bad odors through the nostrils, they spiritually perceive, sense, and discern good and evil through that part of God's Spirit originally breathed into man at creation (see Hebrews 5:14). As the breath (spirit) or the living part of the soul leaves the body the soul goes to sleep.

Scripture indicates the soul (personal identity)[7] goes to hell:[8]

> 7. **Psalms 16:10** *For thou wilt not leave my soul in hell; neither wilt thou suffer thine Holy One to see corruption.* (see also Acts 2:27)[9]

We should bear in mind that graves are pits, and that they are also subterranean (downward, below the surface of the earth, as some Bible translations use the word "nether world" in that text). It also describes a strong demanding or magnetic force

---

[6] The Hebrew word *nashamah* meaning "breath" or "spirit."
[7] The Hebrew word *nephesh* meaning "soul," "mind," "person," or "will."
[8] The Hebrew word *sheol* meaning the "pit" or the "grave."
[9] *Sheol* and *hades* have a parallel meaning. Note that the word *sheol* in Psalms 16:10 is transliterated in its quote in Acts 2:27 with the Greek word *hades*.

(for souls). You may ask, how could the pit, the grave, or the word hell, by definition, mean "demand," or be described as a "magnet for souls?" The answer is in God's decree: *for dust thou art, and unto dust shalt thou return.* (Genesis 3:19). That's why the grave can demand our souls. It is only later that God reversed that decree for those saved from death, where it is written, *...and death and hell* (the grave) *delivered up the dead....* (Revelation 20:13). Jesus stated that God was able to destroy the soul. He indicated this would be in such a place, called hell.

8. **Matthew 10:28** *And fear not them which kill the body, but are not able to kill the soul: but rather fear him which is able to destroy both soul and body in hell.*

The Lord told Moses, David, and many others that they would sleep with their fathers (Deuteronomy 31:16, 2 Samuel 7:12). Stephen is described as falling asleep when he was stoned to death (Acts 7:60). Jesus said that Lazarus was <u>asleep</u>:

9. **John 11:11-13** *These things said he: and after that he saith unto them, Our friend Lazarus sleepeth; but I go, that I may awake him out of sleep. Then said his disciples, Lord, if he sleep, he shall do well. Howbeit Jesus spake of his death: but they thought that he had spoken of taking of rest in sleep.*

"Rest in peace" is an everyday expression that applies to death. "Rest" can refer to resting in a state of sleep. It is often preached that one's mother is rejoicing now in heaven with other departed loved ones because she has gone on to "be with the Lord." The Bible teaches that the dead know not any thing (Ecclesiastes 9:5 and Psalms 146:4).

10. **Isaiah 63:16** *Doubtless thou art our father, though Abraham be ignorant of us, and Israel acknowledge us not....*

The teaching that the departed saved are knowledgeable of anything before the resurrection is a deception. Some say, "I saw my dead grandmother glowing brightly, standing next to my mother's bed while she slept. Grandma turned to me and said that everything was going to be all right. She then floated down the hall never to be seen again". Some say they have even seen Mary, Jesus' mother. This teaching opens the door for familiar spirits, evil spirits/demons, who knew or know, and are familiar with the deceased (and us), to guide people in any direction that they might wish. Job told us <u>when</u> he would live again:

11. **Job 14:10-15** *...man lieth down, and riseth not: till the heavens be no more, they shall not awake, nor be raised out of their sleep. O that thou wouldest hide me in the grave, that thou wouldest keep me secret, until thy wrath be past, that thou wouldest appoint me a set time, and remember me! If a man die, shall he live again? all the days of my appointed time will I wait, till my change come. Thou shalt call, and I will answer thee: thou wilt have a desire to the work of thine hands.*

Those that are passed away have no portion in anything that is done under the sun (see Ecclesiastes 9:6). Do not allow departed "loved ones" to guide you in any direction. The messages may be true, but they will only be true long enough to gain your trust, and then they will deceive. They are <u>not</u> your loved ones, they are evil spirits. Our loved ones that are resting in the Lord do not watch us from heaven, but we can certainly look forward to embracing them again in the world to come.

JESUS WENT TO HELL AND TAUGHT?

It is also taught that Jesus went down to hell and set the captives (in Abraham's bosom) free, then took them to heaven after His death on the cross. This is based on a wrong interpretation of the following scripture:

> 12. **1 Peter 3:18-19** *For Christ also hath once suffered for sins, the just for the unjust, that he might bring us to God, being put to death in the flesh, but quickened by the Spirit: By which also he went and preached unto the spirits in prison;*

Many theologians believe that the idea of being put to death in the flesh refers to the crucifixion of Jesus. Here is their analogy of the event after Jesus' death:

1) Jesus dies on the cross and goes into hell
2) He goes to Abraham's bosom where the departed saved wait for him
3) He preaches to them while He is there
4) He sets them free and takes them to heaven
5) He is resurrected (quickened) by the Holy Spirit

This interpretation is proven to be in error because the above text states that it was "by" that quickened Spirit that he "preached." The order is wrong. The verse shows that he was quickened by the Spirit, which then empowered him to preach and set them free. Let us take a look at what really happened.

After the temptation in the wilderness, Jesus came out in the power of the Spirit. He had overcome the Devil, and had successfully put the flesh to death. He died to those carnal temptations by being _put to death in the flesh_, but _quickened by the Spirit_. Do not miss this point! If anyone has ever experienced being moved mightily by the Spirit of God, then they can testify that their flesh had been put to death in those moments. It was by the Holy Spirit of God that Jesus preached. That same Spirit moved Noah when he was pleading with the people of the earth before the flood. That same Spirit, as Peter stated in 1 Peter 3:20, pleads with souls today to die to the flesh and be baptized, of which the ark of Noah was a type (1 Peter 3:21).

> 13. **Luke 4:14-15** _And Jesus returned in the power of the Spirit into Galilee: and there went out a fame of him through all the region round about. And he taught in their synagogues, being glorified of all._

It must be understood that the synagogues were the prison houses where the people were bound by their traditional doctrines. Many today are being held captive in the same way by their thoughts, and by the ideologies that have been embedded in their minds by books, sermons, and teachings of all kinds. They are held captive by the traditions of their elders. As was then, so it is today. Let us look a little further here, in Luke, to prove the point that these synagogues were those prisons spoken of by Peter.

> 14. **Luke 4:16-21** _And he came to Nazareth, where he had been brought up: and, as his custom was, he went into the synagogue on the sabbath day, and stood up for to read. And there was delivered unto him the book of the prophet Esaias. And when he had opened the book, he found the place where it was written, The Spirit of the_

Lord is upon me, because he hath anointed me to preach the gospel to the poor; he hath sent me to heal the brokenhearted, to preach deliverance to the captives, and recovering of sight to the blind, to set at liberty them that are bruised, To preach the acceptable year of the Lord. And he closed the book, and he gave it again to the minister, and sat down. And the eyes of all them that were in the synagogue were fastened on him. And he began to say unto them, This day is this scripture fulfilled in your ears.

Jesus did that very day what Peter described, not later in the grave! Jesus declared in the synagogue deliverance to captives, the setting at liberty, quoting from Isaiah's statement about the opening of the prison to them that are bound (see Isaiah 61:1, #12), while each person then sat at the edge of their seats to hear what our Lord had to say about that scripture. Jesus then declared that it had <u>just taken place</u> (this day...). It is no wonder that they set out to hurt Him, for He had just declared them blind, bound, and lame. It should be pointed out here that Satan is the <u>prince of darkness</u>, determined to keep, or bind as many as possible within his kingdom (prison). Isaiah 14:17 describes him as the one that *opened <u>not</u> the house of his prisoners.* In Hebrew, this verse might be better translated: "who did not let his prisoners (the deceived) loose homewards (heavenward, or into the kingdom).

So this is the order that Peter speaks of:

1) Jesus was put to death in the flesh by killing the desires of the flesh during his forty days in the wilderness. Romans 8:13 states: *For if ye live after the flesh, ye shall die: but if ye through the Spirit do mortify the deeds of the body, ye shall live.*

27

2) Jesus was quickened by the Spirit. Romans 8:14 states: *For as many as are led by the Spirit of God, they are the sons of God.*

3) Jesus came out of the wilderness in the power of the Spirit to preach to those that were bound (in prisons, i.e. synagogues) by traditions and false doctrines. Luke 4:21 states: *And he began to say unto them, This day is this scripture fulfilled in your ears.*

4) Jesus set them free from the darkness, false teachings, and wrongdoing. John 8:32-36 states: *And ye shall know the truth, and the truth shall make you free. They answered him, We be Abraham's seed, and were never in bondage to any man: how sayest thou, Ye shall be made free? Jesus answered them, Verily, verily, I say unto you, Whomsoever committeth sin is the servant of sin. And the servant abideth not in the house for ever: but the Son abideth forever. If the Son therefore shall make you free, ye shall be free indeed.*

Romans 6:11 states: *Likewise reckon ye also yourselves to be dead indeed unto sin,* (every day of your Christian walk*), but alive* (quickened) *unto God through Jesus Christ our Lord.* If we can be dead to sin, and quickened unto God during our lifetime then we can preach truth which will set many free from Satan's lies, just as Jesus did during His lifetime, not in hell! (See Romans 6:6-7, 18).

Others might believe that Jesus went into hell to preach by using the verse: *Now that he ascended, what was it but that he also descended first into the lower parts of the earth?* (Ephesians 4:9). Yet this only speaks of his being born in a manger, and having nowhere to lay his head (Luke 9:58). The shepherds that found him lying in a manger understood that he came from the highest realm to exist in a lower state than everyone else (being born in a manger in a state of poverty, and later to be smitten of God, as stated in Isaiah 53:4). Had Jesus come to be born in a palace, many of the poor may have felt that he did not come to save the poorest of the poor. Our Lord stooped down in humility to lift us all up to him. Praise him evermore!

WHO DOES JESUS RAISE FROM THE DEAD?

Jesus said that all that are in the graves shall hear his voice, but, he also stated that it was <u>his sheep</u> that hear his voice. That is correct, as the scripture tells us that the wicked (ungodly) <u>will not rise</u>!

15. **John 5:25** *Verily, verily, I say unto you, The hour is coming, and now is, when the dead shall hear the voice of the Son of God: and they that hear shall live.*

16. **Isaiah 26:14** *They are dead, they shall not live; they are deceased, they shall not rise: therefore hast thou visited and destroyed them, and made all their memory to perish.*

17. **Jeremiah 51:39** *In their heat I will make their feasts, and I will make them drunken, that they may rejoice, and sleep a perpetual sleep, and not wake, saith the LORD.*

18. **Psalms 36:12** *There are the workers of iniquity fallen: they are cast down, and shall not be able to rise.*

19. **Psalms 140:10** *Let burning coals fall upon them:* (this is their punishment that they experience <u>before</u> death) *let them be cast into the fire;* (experience God's wrath) *into deep pits, that they rise* (awaken) *not up again.*

Wait a minute! What about the second resurrection? Don't most Christians teach that the wicked will "stand before God" as seen in Revelation 20:13, at the great white throne judgment, when the sea, death, and hell deliver up the dead which were in them? Yes, that is what they teach (that the lost and the wicked will rise and stand before God to be judged), but Psalm 1:5 states that the wicked shall not <u>stand</u>[10] in judgement:

> 20. **Psalms 1:5** *Therefore the ungodly shall not stand in the judgment, nor sinners in the congregation of the righteous.*

John the Baptist made reference to this point as he was preaching to the multitudes about standing and hearing the voice of the bridegroom (John 3:29). Let us look further:

> 21. **John 3:36** *He that believeth on the Son hath everlasting life: and he that believeth not the Son shall not see life; but the wrath of God abideth on him.*

This is found elsewhere in scripture:

> 22. **John 11:25** *Jesus said unto her, I am the resurrection, and the life: he that believeth in me, though he were dead, yet shall he live:*

Jesus often indicated in the scripture that one <u>must</u> believe in him to see life in the resurrection.

> 23. **John 5:21** *For as the Father raiseth up the dead, and quickeneth them; even so the Son quickeneth whom he will.*

> 24. **John 6:39-40** *And this is the Father's will which hath*

---

[10] The Hebrew word ***quwm*** meaning "to rise up."

sent me, that of all which he hath given me I should lose nothing, but should raise it up again at the last day. And this is the will of him that sent me, that every one which seeth the Son, and believeth on him, may have everlasting life: and I will raise him up at the last day.

Let us take that a little further…

25. **John 6:44** *No man can come to me, except the Father which hath sent me draw him: and I will raise him up at the last day.*

26. **Hebrews 5:9** *And being made perfect, he became the author of eternal salvation unto all them that obey him;*

27. **1 John 5:12** *He that hath the Son hath life; and he that hath not the Son of God hath not life.*

28. **Mark 12:26-27** *And as touching the dead, that they rise: have ye not read in the book of Moses, how in the bush God spake unto him, saying, I am the God of Abraham, and the God of Isaac, and the God of Jacob? He is <u>not the God of the dead</u>, but the God of the living: ye therefore do <u>greatly</u> err.* (Look again at #27 as to <u>who</u> the living are).

Paul spoke of this in regard to those who are truly alive! The "all" he referred to are believers in Christ (#27 and 29). The dead that God is not the God of are the children of the Devil, for they never made the Lord their God. These are the dead that need to bury their dead (Luke 9:60).

29. **1 Timothy 5:6** *But she that liveth in pleasure is dead while she liveth.*

30. **Romans 6:10** *For in that he died, he died unto sin once: but in that he liveth, he liveth unto God.*

31. **Luke 20:34-38** *And Jesus answering said unto them, The children of this world marry, and are given in marriage: But they which <u>shall</u> be accounted <u>worthy to obtain</u> that world, and* (to obtain) <u>*the resurrection from the dead*</u>*, neither marry, nor are given in marriage: Neither can they die any more: for they are equal unto the angels; and are the children of God, being the children of the resurrection* (this refers to the first resurrection). *Now that the dead are raised, even Moses shewed at the bush, when he calleth the Lord the God of Abraham, and the God of Isaac, and the God of Jacob. For he is not a God of the dead, but of the living: for all* (saved) *live unto him.*

God loves us far beyond what our finite minds can understand. He created us so that we could experience eternal joy with Him. Nothing on earth is worth risking missing out on all that, and all we have do to is choose life.

SPOKEN OUT OF EXISTENCE

Have I not said that the scriptures indicate that some will not stand (rise) in the judgement? Does that mean that they will no longer exist at that point of time? Don't people teach that some will live forever burning, sizzling, crackling, and in agony throughout eternity in hell? I resist the teaching of the traditional doctrine of <u>living</u> in eternal damnation. The following scriptures will show that the wicked will be spoken out of existence at death because they did not choose life. They did not choose the blessing, but instead chose the curse (Deuteronomy 30:19-20), and rejected the plan of salvation which would have saved them from death.

> 33. **Obadiah 1:16** *For as ye have drunk upon my holy mountain, so shall all the heathen drink continually, yea, they shall drink, and they shall swallow down, and they shall be as though they had not been.*

> 34. **Ezekiel 26:21** *I will make thee a terror, and thou shalt be no more: though thou be sought for, yet shalt thou never be found again, saith the Lord GOD.*

> 35. **Proverbs 10:25** *As the whirlwind passeth, <u>so is the wicked no more</u>: but the righteous is an everlasting foundation.*

> 36. **Romans 6:23** *For the wages of sin is death; but the gift of God is eternal life through Jesus Christ our Lord.*

Wait a minute. Is it not our understanding that Satan would be punished forever? Well, he <u>will</u> be. How? He will be spoken out of existence. That is forever! The Bible says eternal punishment, not eternal punishing! One is eternally punished when he or she is destroyed; spoken out of existence, to be no more. That is eternal judgement for the wicked, the unrepentant, and the ungodly.

Consider a house that catches on fire. Let's say that this house burns to the ground. It no longer exists. You can not change that, it is forever! Yet the burning does not last forever. Now imagine that it is put out at some point. Either way, what happened to the house cannot be changed.

Compare that burning house to a person that experiences the wrath of God. The fire could either cause one to repent, to become a better humble Christian, or it could cause that person to become bitter, in which case he will be totally consumed in his iniquity, like being burned to ashes. The Bible teaches that God is a consuming fire (Deuteronomy 4:24, Hebrews 12:29) that shall not be quenched.

37. **Ezekiel 22:21-22** *Yea, I will gather you, and blow upon you in the fire of my wrath, and ye shall be melted in the midst thereof. As silver is melted in the midst of the furnace, so shall ye be melted in the midst thereof; and ye shall know that I the LORD have poured out my fury upon you.*

38. **2 Chronicles 34:25** *Because they have forsaken me, and have burned incense unto other gods, that they might provoke me to anger with all the works of their hands; therefore my wrath shall be poured out upon this place, and shall not be quenched.*

Here, God's wrath would be poured out upon Judah, and would not be quenched. Fire could represent war, pestilence, famine, or even "hell on earth," but the result is that it will bring death, never to change (shall not be quenched). The consuming fire <u>destroys</u>. (See Deuteronomy 32:20-26).

39. **Deuteronomy 9:3** *Understand therefore this day, that the LORD thy God is he which goeth over before thee; as a consuming fire he shall destroy them, and he shall bring them down before thy face: so shalt thou drive them out, and destroy them quickly, as the LORD hath said unto thee.*

Satan and his demons will be exposed to God's wrath in this destructive way. Even though one may say that the above verse only applies to mortal death, and could not imply the destruction of the soul, I would like to call attention to the following verses that show that Satan and his fallen angels will be destroyed, yea, <u>spoken out</u> of existence.

40. **Ezekiel 28:14-19** *...I will cast thee as profane out of the mountain of God: and <u>I will destroy thee</u>, O covering cherub, from the midst of the stones of fire. Thine heart was lifted up because of thy beauty, thou hast corrupted thy wisdom by reason of thy brightness: I will cast thee to the ground, I will lay thee before kings, that they may behold thee. Thou hast defiled thy sanctuaries by the multitude of thine iniquities, by the iniquity of thy traffick; therefore will <u>I bring forth a fire from the midst of thee</u>, it shall devour thee, and <u>I will bring thee to ashes upon the earth</u> in the sight of all them that behold thee. All they that know thee among the people shall be astonished at thee: thou shalt be a terror, and <u>never shalt thou be any more</u>.*

41. **Hebrews 2:14** *Forasmuch then as the children are partakers of flesh and blood, he also himself likewise took part of the same; that through death <u>he might destroy him</u> that had the power of death, that is, the devil;*

42. **Luke 4:33–34** *And in the synagogue there was a man, which had a spirit of an unclean devil, and cried out with a loud voice, Saying, Let us alone; what have we to do with thee, thou Jesus of Nazareth? <u>art thou come to destroy us?</u> I know thee who thou art; the Holy One of God.*

43. **Psalms 9:3–6** *When mine enemies are turned back, they shall fall and perish at thy presence. For thou hast maintained my right and my cause; thou satest in the throne judging right. Thou hast rebuked the heathen, <u>thou hast destroyed the wicked</u>, thou hast put out their name for ever and ever. O thou enemy, <u>destructions are come to a perpetual end</u>: and thou hast destroyed cities; <u>their memorial is perished with them</u>.*

44. **Ezekiel 18:4** *Behold, all souls are mine; as the soul of the father, so also the soul of the son is mine: <u>the soul that sinneth, it shall die</u>.*

45. **Psalms 13:3** *Consider and hear me, O LORD my God: lighten mine eyes, lest I sleep the sleep of death;*

HELL VERSUS THE LAKE OF FIRE

Many people believe that *sheol* is the lake of fire, the place of God's wrath. If you research this Hebrew word, you will find that most Bible versions insert the word "grave" whenever the Hebrew word *sheol* appeared in the underlying Hebrew text. To illustrate my point, ask yourself why Job would request to be hid in God's wrath (*sheol*) until His wrath would be past.

> 46. **Job 14:13** *O that thou wouldest <u>hide me</u> in the grave (**sheol**), that thou wouldest keep me secret, until thy wrath be past, that thou wouldest appoint me a set time, and remember me!*

This is why the definition of the word *sheol* includes the idea of a subterranean <u>retreat</u> i.e. "hide me."

Many feel that "hell" is synonymous with the lake of fire. If this is so, how can the lake of fire be thrown into the lake of fire?

> 47. **Revelation 20:14** *And death and hell were cast into the lake of fire. This is the second death.*

Notice that this verse states that *this is the second death*. Not only will the last enemy, Death, be destroyed as it is stated in 1 Corinthians 15:26 and here in Revelation, but hell, or the grave, the place where the wicked <u>remain</u>, shall also be destroyed, made non-existent.

> 48. **Psalms 37:10** *For yet a little while, and the wicked shall not be: yea, thou shalt diligently consider <u>his place</u>, and it <u>shall not be</u>.*

DOES NOT INTERPRETATION BELONG TO GOD?

I have a friend that was having a hard time accepting the things presented in this exposition. This is what Solomon meant by his advice to *Buy the truth...* (Proverbs 23:23). We sometimes have to pay a great price wrestling (perhaps for months) with doctrine. Traditional teaching, having been learned over a longer period of time, causes us to need time; time to realize that it is false, and to accept the truth. The price is high, because it hurts in the <u>pit of our stomachs</u> when we realize that we have adhered to a lie (that bitterness in the belly).

Solomon also said to: *Sell it* (the truth) *not*. This indicates that it is often easier to settle for something that is not true, because the price of humbling oneself to say (or possibly teach) that we were wrong is just too high to pay. If that price is too high to pay, then the truth is "sold off" for something that is cheaper, or easier to accept, easier to live with, easier to deal with in respect to what the flock is taught. To some ministers, the idea of standing before their flocks and teaching something that may take months to learn is frightful. They may even fear that half of their congregation will get up and walk out on them because of the truth (see John 6:66). That minister just might take the cost free route and ignore the truth that he has learned on this subject. He won't take any steps toward releasing the prisoners of <u>traditional teaching</u>. That kind of minister will in effect be taking the mark of the beast, because he would be allowing his flock to believe a lie, and to be "marked" in their foreheads (minds) with false teachings. That kind of minister will not only sell out on his flock, but he also would have sold the truth. One who will not accept Gods' truth, who will follow human traditions instead, in thought and deed, is marked "in the forehead" (mind) and in the right hand of fellowship (deed).

My friend studied the subject by searching the scriptures and letting God lead him through to the truth. Let me return to my friend, and how God helped him a little later.

THE ART OF GEMATRIA

Many languages have a numeric equivalence assigned to each of their letters. This is one of the ways that the Hebrew Rabbis would use to assure accurate copying of scripture texts. They would take the value of each letter, total the sum of the word, and then find the total sum of the entire page they were copying. If the total on the scroll being copied was equal to the value of that just written, then they were fully assured the copy was accurate.

The alphabets of different languages have different gematria. An example of this is the alphabetical assignments of Roman numerals: I=1, V=5, X=1O, L=50, C=1OO, and D=500. Add these base numerals up and their sum is 666.

The Greek word for "tradition" is **paradosi**. The numeric equivalence for each letter of this word gives a total sum of the word as 666! Keep in mind that Greek letter values differed from the values of Roman letters.

Alpha Character	Numeric Value
P	80
A	1
R	100
A	1
D	4
O	70
S	200
I	10
S	200
Total Value	666

Again, Jesus said in **Mark 7:9** ...*Full well ye reject the commandment of God* (the truth), *that ye may keep* (cling to) *your own tradition* (666). It is no wonder it is a mark, or a branding in the forehead, the mind won't let it go (it clings to it).

My friend soon came to realize just how wide the gate (mouth) of destruction had become through traditional teachings, and that hell (destruction and deception) had indeed enlarged herself (Isaiah 5:14). It receives many who unwittingly stand against the truth and against those who hold to it. They are actually opposing themselves (2 Timothy 2:5). The above example shows how human traditions equate with the "mark of the beast" found in Revelation, for it is the number of man, or man's teachings.

People who follow traditions not in accordance with God's word and the Bible, who believe the traditions in word, thought, and deed, are marked in the forehead and hands (see Revelation 13:16), for they adhere to the ways of man, not the ways of God. Almost all of the people who thought they understood the scriptures in the days of Christ felt that his teachings were strange doctrine. Most of the people of the church in the approaching days of his second coming will also find that the "church" of Christ is again in a mess. Why? Because most of the Christian church has been misled in many of their doctrines. One must consider that the true church in the early days was a complete contradiction to just about everything that was in existence.

As my friend was paying the price of letting go (or trying to let go) of all of his pre-programmed thoughts regarding eternal judgment, he asked <u>God</u> to show him the truth. The next day he told me of this petition and that he had received a dream. In the dream he was in a house. There was water coming into the house like a flood. As the waters continued to rise, he tried to salvage things that were in the house. He said that the water was very dirty. The dirty water signifies <u>the people of the world</u> that are "the <u>dirty sea of humanity</u>".

The next day, I called my pastor. I told him Revelation 20:10 showed that Satan would be tormented forever and ever, which appears to contradict scriptures that foretells his extinction. He said that if I simply went a little further to Revelation 21, I would find the answer.

49. **Revelation 21:4** *And God shall wipe away all tears from their eyes; and there shall be no more death, neither sorrow, nor crying, neither shall there be any more pain: for the former things are passed away.*

This verse states that there will be no sorrow or pain. It will be over and gone. It will no longer exist, period! As all the things that God does away with will be gone, including the grave, death, and hell, this condition of torment will be gone, nonexistent, as one of those former things that are passed away! I then went back to the first verse of this chapter to find something that struck a familiar note.

50. **Revelation 21:1** *And I saw a new heaven and a new earth: for the first heaven and the first earth were passed away; and there was <u>no more sea</u>.*

I then found a reference in my Bible that led me to the following scripture:

> 51. **Isaiah 57:20** *But the wicked are like the troubled sea, when it cannot rest, whose waters cast up mire and dirt.*

The wicked, compared to the <u>troubled</u> sea, cannot rest. There is no <u>peace</u> (lack of rest) for the wicked. This verse calls the wicked a troubled sea, synonymous with dirty waters. The word of God explained the dream. <u>The wicked</u> (the troubled sea as a flood) shall be no more: *and there was no more sea.* God showed my friend the dirty waters rising to flood the land. In the last days, the wicked will flood this earth with wave after wave of destruction, until all the wicked will have destroyed one another. Then God's word indicates that the wicked will be no more. They will no longer <u>exist</u>. Since they will not <u>exist</u>, then we know that eternal life in agony is false. They will no longer exist. The pain will no longer <u>exist</u>, sorrow will no longer <u>exist</u>! The word of God proves it. This dream <u>had to be based</u> on the Word of God, and it was! Dreams, visions, and other forms of revelation <u>must be</u> scripturally sound. If a person's dream or vision does not measure up to the word of God, than it is a deception of the Devil, or a product of the person's own false preconceptions. He was then settled in his heart that this was truth, for he asked <u>God</u> to show him, and he now felt that at this point, God, <u>through a dream and His word</u>, had honored his request.

Of course God will have to help settle this in your heart as well, provided that this is true, and that you deal with this subject and yourself honestly.

Perhaps one should examine the truth found in many hymns, such as this piece written by James Rowe and Howard Smith in 1912:

<u>Love Lifted Me</u>
I was sinking deep in sin, far from the peaceful shore:
very deeply stained within, sinking to <u>rise no more...</u>
But the Master of the sea, heard my despairing cry,
<u>from the waters</u> lifted me, now safe am I.

WHY THE LIE?

Before the Garden of Eden, Satan was full of wisdom and perfect in beauty (Ezekiel 28:12). With this kind of glory, pride set in, and he wanted to be worshipped also (Ezekiel 28:17, Isaiah 14:12-14).

Since his defeat in heaven (Revelation 12:7-9), Satan has tried to hurt God by destroying those that God loves. Misery loves company. God speaks of His own tears often in scripture (Jeremiah 9:1-3, 4:19, Isaiah 1:11-15). Satan wants to hurt both us and God.

It must always be remembered that Satan's primary goal is to get those that are lost to reject God when they hear His word. Many people reject God because the thought of Him subjecting them to an eternal place where they would sizzle and crackle in agony endlessly is too great. One religion declares that there is a tree in the midst of hell (this lie is an imitation of the tree in the midst of Eden). From this tree, boiling sap drips forth to which people in hell run to catch some drops on their tongues. It is taught that this sap is so hot that it burns through their mouth and throats to the point of near destruction, yet the people are willing to drink of it thinking it will put them out of their misery, only God will not let them perish.

What kind of an impression does this false teaching give people of what God is like? Does this sound like the God that declares in Psalms 145:9 that mercy is over all His works? Satan wants people to see God as one that declares, "It is my way or else I will make you pay: yea, regret it throughout eternity." Satan

49

wants to depict God as a God of wrath without mercy. Many have refused to accept God because of this distorted description. But the Bible says:

52. **Habakkuk 3:2** *O LORD, I have heard thy speech, and was afraid: O LORD, revive thy work in the midst of the years, in the midst of the years make known; <u>in wrath remember mercy.</u>*

THE FIRE OF HELL

53. **Psalms 75:6** *For promotion cometh neither from the east, nor from the west, nor from the south.*

When we read this verse we can see that east, west, and south are places where promotion does not come from. That leaves only the north. This is where promotion does come from (many times God expects us to think, to use our heads, to read between the lines, in order to understand what He is saying).

To understand that promotion comes from the north, we should know what "north" points to. This is not directional north, as in the North Pole. This is speaking of celestial north (like looking up into heaven at the North Star). In essence it is saying that promotion comes from above, or from heaven (from God).

54. **Proverbs 18:16** *A man's gift maketh room for him, and bringeth him before great men.*

55. **Daniel 2:37** *Thou, O king, art a king of kings: for the God of heaven hath given thee a kingdom, power, and strength, and glory.*

The gift referred to in both verses above is the promotion of man by God. If you were on the other side of the world, where would heaven be? It is still upward. So heaven, being upward, no matter where you are standing on the earth, reaches out into space and beyond. Thus heaven is <u>anywhere</u> in the entire universe except for the planet Earth.

The Bible says that Satan was in <u>heaven</u> before his fall (Revelation 12:3, Isaiah 14:12, and Ezekiel 28:14), and that he was cast <u>down</u> to the ground (Ezekiel 28:17), which means cast out of heaven into the Earth. So we see here that Satan could go anywhere in heaven, except its <u>highest</u> parts (Isaiah 14:12-13). He is now restricted to this little planet known as Earth. You might say that Satan is now incarcerated, restricted to a very small space compared to the vast territory that he used to roam.

We have also seen that God has declared in His word that <u>Satan will be destroyed</u>. The gavel has been dropped, and the sentence has been issued. Judgment has been passed on Satan and he now awaits his execution. Can you imagine that? It is like being on death row without the slightest possibility of a stay of execution. Many death row inmates, after being taken off of death row before they were executed, testified that being on death row was like a living hell. Satan is doomed to destruction, and there is not a single thing he can do about it. He waits in the small confinement of this planet until his death. This has to be a terrible feeling. The Serpent, who's <u>pride</u> was his downfall, has now been humiliated before the entire universe. He has been given certain powers, but every time he tries to move out of his bounds, he is jerked back on a leash of chains by God. He also must look into heaven to see the Son of God, Jesus Christ, sitting on the right hand of the Father.

Believe it or not, Satan is <u>now</u> in torment <u>night and day</u>, burning in his own self, living in the hell that he has brought upon himself. This will continue until the day of his destruction. His angels are reserved in everlasting chains of darkness (misery, sorrow, and ignorance) until that day comes (see Jude 6). He knows that he has only a short time remaining (see Revelation 12:12).

Some people may feel that such a punishment, to be spoken out of existence, sounds great compared to what they previously thought hell was like. That in itself tells me that they are deceived. Walking blindly into destruction with an attitude of "partying until 1999" is just what Satan wants. You can be assured of this: Satan fears destruction (knowing nothing) very, very much! He has existed for <u>over</u> six thousand years. Life is worth little to him now, in the miserable form it has taken, but at least it <u>is</u> life. This is why he wants to believe that *Ye shalt <u>not</u> surely die.*

So the fire of hell is the punishment that one suffers for disobedience to God. It is like being engulfed in the consuming wrath of God, in whatever form that punishment takes. Satan has been going through this punishment for thousands of years. He has brought this "hell" upon himself. Now, think very carefully about this next statement. This punishment that Satan has been going through is a <u>severe</u> punishment compared to the quick extinction of the people of Sodom and Gomorrah. Even Israel's punishment has lasted two thousand years. Would you rather suffer one day's destruction, or a lifetime knowing that God has turned His back on you as He has Satan? The more knowledge one has, the more the severity of the punishment. This is why people believe that there are measures of punishment.

56. **Luke 12:47-48** *And that servant* (as Satan once was), *which knew his lord's will, and prepared not himself, neither did according to his will, shall be beaten with many stripes. But he that knew not* (like the people of Sodom), *and did commit things worthy of stripes, shall be beaten with few stripes. For unto whomsoever much is given, of him shall be much required: and to whom men have committed much, of him they will ask the more.*

It should be understood that the fire of hell is God's judgment upon a person or <u>nation</u> because of disobedience. This punishment may bring about repentance as we are about to see. In such a case it is compared to that house that caught fire, but was put out before it was completely destroyed. Let us look at a perfect example of what the cleansing fire can do.

LAZARUS AND THE RICH MAN
National punishment

We have seen that torment night and day is something that Satan has come to know well. This is because he knew the Lord's will, but refused to do it. The nation of Israel was given the word of God, but they consistently refused to take heed to it. This is why God has temporarily turned his back on that nation.

57. **Luke 16:19-31** *There was a certain rich man, which was clothed in purple and fine linen, and fared sumptuously every day: And there was a certain beggar named Lazarus, which was laid at his gate, full of sores, And desiring to be fed with the crumbs which fell from the rich man's table: moreover the dogs came and licked his sores. And it came to pass, that the beggar died, and was carried by the angels into Abraham's bosom: the rich man also died, and was buried; And in hell he lift up his eyes, being in torments, and seeth Abraham afar off, and Lazarus in his bosom. And he cried and said, Father Abraham, have mercy on me, and send Lazarus, that he may dip the tip of his finger in water, and cool my tongue; for I am tormented in this flame. But Abraham said, Son, remember that thou in thy lifetime receivedst thy good things, and likewise Lazarus evil things: but now he is comforted, and thou art tormented. And beside all this, between us and you there is a great gulf fixed: so that they which would pass from hence to you cannot; neither can they pass to us, that would come from thence. Then he said, I pray thee therefore, father, that thou wouldest send him to my father's house: For I have five brethren; that he may testify unto them, lest they also come into this place of torment. Abraham saith unto him, They have Moses and the prophets; let them hear them. And he*

said, Nay, father Abraham: but if one went unto them from the dead, they will repent. And he said unto him, If they hear not Moses and the prophets, neither will they be persuaded, though one rose from the dead.

This is what is seen in the parable of Lazarus and the rich man. Now I am aware that many say that this is not a parable, because of the fact that the text never declares it to be a parable. If one looks at Luke 15:3, it says *He* (Jesus) *spake this parable unto them....* He then began to speak of the shepherd that leaves the ninety-nine sheep to find the one that was lost. His next words describe the woman that found a piece of lost silver, followed by the "Prodigal Son" who was lost and found. Consider the fact that the story of the woman, the prodigal son, and even the unjust steward of the next chapter were never declared to be parables. To cancel out the possibility that the story of Lazarus and the rich man is a parable for that reason does not hold any water, because the aforementioned examples were not referred to directly as parables either, though all would consider them to be so.

Another reason that people believe that this is not a parable is because there are no parables in the scriptures using a person's name. By <u>whose</u> rules are they <u>playing</u> with?! Who ever said that using a person's name in a parable is taboo, or against God's ways? This too does not hold water.

The fact is, this <u>is</u> a parable, as you are about to see. The name "Lazarus" is the same name seen in the Old Testament, only it appears as Eleazar. This is because of transliteration, which is often found in the translation of one language into another. One example of this is the word "shekel," which is a weight used in the balances of the temple. This word is transliterated as the word "tekel" in Daniel 5:27. This also occurs in the case of names. Jonah is transliterated as Jonas in the New Testament. Isaiah is transliterated as Esaias. Elijah is transliterated as Elias, and Hosea as Osee. The name Lazarus (Eleazar) means "God is my helper, my aid, my protector."

Jesus stated that the rich man's brothers would not be persuaded even though one rose from the dead. Most people misunderstand the fact that this speaks of the Jews who would not believe in Christ as the Messiah, even if he (pictured by Lazarus in this parable) was to rise from the dead. Let us look at this from that perspective to see if we can hear what God is saying to the nation of Israel:

58. **Luke 16:19** *There was a certain rich man, which was clothed in purple and fine linen, and fared sumptuously every day:*

The "rich man" represents the nation of Israel, for they were very rich with the favor and blessings of God, like no other nation on earth. The purple speaks of the royal bloodline of the Jews as God's people, the bloodline from which the Savior of the world would be born. The fine linen speaks of the forgiveness that the nation (as a whole) continually received, for that fine linen covers the nakedness (shame of guilt) when standing before God. Even after all the disobedience in Israel's past, God declared through Balaam's prophecy in **Numbers 23:21** *He hath not beheld iniquity in Jacob, neither hath he seen perverseness in Israel: the LORD his God is with him, and the shout of a king is among them.*

59. **Luke 16:20** *And there was a certain beggar named Lazarus, which was laid at his gate, full of sores,*

This is where people's eyes seem to be closed. They recognized the rejection of that person who would rise from the grave as the rejection of Christ, but they forget that it was <u>this</u> man, <u>Lazarus</u>, that was the person requested to be sent back from the dead. <u>Jesus</u> was that beggar, in that he begged the Jewish nation to accept the gospel. Laying at the gate of the rich man signifies the idea that he stands at the door and knocks: and if any man hears his voice, and opens the door, he would come in to him, and would sup with him, and he with Jesus (see Revelation 3:20). Being full of sores expresses the pain that <u>anyone</u> sharing the gospel would feel for the lost when they reject the extended hand of mercy held out by the Lord.

60. **Luke 16:21** *And desiring to be fed with the crumbs which fell from the rich man's table: moreover the dogs came and licked his sores.*

Desiring to be fed with the crumbs displays the humble attitude one has when pleading that another receive the gospel of Christ (see Mark 1:15). Dogs are known to have an antibacterial agent in their saliva. This is where the expression comes from that one is "licking their wounds." The wounds that are licked by a dog have a strong chance of not getting infected. The dogs that came and licked <u>his</u> wounds are the sinners, harlots, publicans, and others that took the pain of rejection away by accepting eternal life through his Word. It surely is a painful thing when one mocks a Christian who hazards his or her very own life for the eternal sake of the person doing the mocking. This is what

Job meant by the statement that people gnashed upon him with their teeth (see Job 16:9, Psalm 31:12, and Matthew 27:44). Job was saying that it hurt, or caused sores. Any witness of God knows that <u>almost all</u> the pain of rejection <u>this</u> world has to offer can be taken away by those few, if even only one, who accepts eternal life through Christ. The pain of rejection by the Jewish nation was "healed or soothed" by the few who accepted Him.

> 61. **Luke 16:22** *And it came to pass, that the beggar died, and was carried by the angels into Abraham's bosom: the rich man also died, and was buried;*

It appears as though the death of the beggar is brought on by the rejection, or neglect, of the rich man, and so it was. The Jewish nation rejected Christ, a rejection which ultimately had caused His death. The parable states that <u>Jesus is in the bosom of the Father</u> (John 1:18), who, in these verses is pictured as Lazarus and Father Abraham. Jesus used parabolic language to express the <u>Jewish</u> view that association with Abraham (and to be in his bosom) signified being in a state of favor with God. Jesus stated that Lazarus had God's blessings, but that the rich man did not. We know that Jesus was carried away in the clouds into heaven to be seated on his Father's right hand. The death of the rich man signifies that the nation of Israel (that generation) died in their sins.

Now here is the heart of the parable, one of the primary points that God is expressing to the nation of Israel. This will take some time to consider. This directly relates to the fact that Israel is going to reap what they have sown, in that they are going to receive many stripes for not doing the Lord's will, after having known His will. This is the house that burns until it is put out, and which happens to be the house of Israel. This house does not completely perish because there is repentance as we will soon see. This burning is the punishment that God places on Israel. This burning punishment is to last for two thousand years.

In Jerusalem, the <u>temple court</u> was two thousand cubits. This is where the <u>Gentiles</u> were permitted to go, by grace, as prophesied in **Genesis 9:27** *...Japheth...shall dwell in the tents of Shem.* This is the dispensation of grace, the period of time in which God has turned His back on Israel as a nation, and has turned to the Gentiles. This period of grace will last for two thousand years, (the details of which we will discuss later). This period is known as a **separation period** between the nation of Israel and God. It is seen in this parable as the great **gulf** between Lazarus (Christ) and the rich man (Israel).

> 62. **Hosea 5:15** *I will go and return to my place, <u>till they acknowledge their offence</u>, and seek my face: in their affliction they will seek me early.*

This affliction will last for two thousand years, starting with the rejection (offense), as the persecution from their enemies will increase in the last days. The <u>next </u>chapter in Hosea picks up on the same thought, as the nation of Israel <u>does</u> repent by admitting their responsibility for the death of Christ (Lazarus):

> 63. **Hosea 6:1-2** *Come, and let us return unto the LORD: for he hath torn, and he will heal us; he hath smitten, and he will bind us*

up. <u>*After two days*</u> (two thousand years) *will he revive us: in the third day* <u>*he will raise us up*</u> (a national resurrection pictured by the dry bones in Ezekiel 37), *and we shall live in his sight* (live in obedience before him).

The Ark of the Covenant was a type (an Old Testament symbolic picture) of Christ. The <u>presence</u> of the Ark signified the presence of God.

64. **Joshua 3:4** *Yet there shall be a space between you and it, about two thousand cubits by measure: come not near unto it, that ye may know* (learn) <u>*the way*</u> *by which ye must go:* (learn that he will have mercy and grace) *for ye have not passed this way heretofore.*

Jesus stated that the sign of Jonah would be given to the nation of Israel; that he, the Son of man, in the belly of the earth, would be like Jonah in the belly of the whale (see Matthew 12:40). This is also a type of what the <u>scriptures</u> indicated would happen to the <u>entire nation</u> of Israel. We know of Jesus being in the belly of the earth, but let us look again at Jonah:

65. **Jonah 2:2** *And said, I cried by* <u>*reason of mine affliction*</u> *unto the LORD, and he heard me; out of* <u>*the belly of hell*</u> *cried I, and thou heardest my voice.*

Now let us look at how God said this would apply to the entire nation of Israel:

66. **Hosea 8:8** *Israel is swallowed up: now shall they be among the Gentiles as a vessel wherein is no pleasure.*

We know that the whale spit Jonah up, and the grave (hell) "gave up" the Lord. The punishment on the nation of Israel will end when the Gentile (leviathan) powers come to an end. As they begin their attempt to destroy (afflict) Israel in the last days, the Gentiles of this last day will spit out Israel as they become disgusted with the taste of Israel's God. The whale vomited Jonah up, and God will raise Israel up, like saying that one "<u>brought up</u>" his lunch.

Jonah was the only Old Testament prophet sent to a Gentile nation with a message from God. Jonah did not want to go (see Jonah 1:3). Israel, rich and living off of the fat of the land, only looked down on the Gentiles, and lacked the desire to see them benefit from God. Israel saw no purpose in carrying a message to the Gentile world, so the <u>nation</u> was swallowed up, just like Jonah, the prophet who represented them. Israel needed to learn the way of God's grace. Much like Jonah and the prodigal son's brother, they were prejudiced. Notice how both those stories end on a negative note. The prophet Jonah, the prodigal's brother, and the nation of Israel had yet to "learn the way by which they must go" (they must learn grace). That is where the Courtyard, where the Gentiles can dwell in the tents of Shem, comes in. It is the period of grace, lasting two thousand years (equal to its measurement in cubits, and symbolically to the great gulf), a hard lesson to be "learned" by the nation.

At the close of this millennium, after these two days (two thousand years since the rejection of Christ), the third day will follow. God will <u>raise them up</u> out of their "hell," like a valley of dry bones that need moisture to live (see Ezekiel 37:1-14).

67. **Jonah 2:6** *I went down to the bottoms of the mountains; the earth with her <u>bars</u> was about me for ever: yet hast thou <u>brought up</u> my life from corruption, O LORD my God.*

So Israel will repent, but what brings that about? Punishment!

68. **Psalms 119:71** *It is good for me that I have been afflicted; that I might learn thy statutes.*

69. **Psalms 119:59** *I thought on my ways, and turned my feet unto thy testimonies.*

History shows that Israel has suffered greatly since the rejection of Christ. The Jews are viewed by the world as very materialistic. This is because as a nation (not including the few that were blessed to be saved), they have had nothing else to live for except for what this material world has to offer. Knowing that God has turned His back on a person causes life to be miserable. Israel has tasted of God's judgement for two thousand years, a living hell, a lake of fire. Look at how this state of being "down in the pits" looks much like a lake.

70. **Jonah 2:3** *For thou hadst cast me into the deep, in the midst of the seas; and the floods compassed me about: all thy billows and thy waves passed over me.*

71. **Psalms 88:4-7** *I am counted with them that go down into the pit: I am as a man that hath no strength: Free among the dead, <u>like the slain that lie in the grave, whom thou rememberest no more</u>: and they are cut off from thy hand. Thou hast laid me in the lowest pit, in darkness, in the deeps. Thy wrath lieth hard upon me,*

and thou hast afflicted me with all thy waves. Selah.

Affliction causes one to come to their senses, like the prodigal son waking up and smelling the coffee.

> 72. **Luke 15:17** *And when he came to himself, he said, How many hired servants of my father's have bread enough and to spare, and I perish with hunger!*

> 73. **Jonah 2:7** *When my soul fainted within me I remembered the LORD: and my prayer came in unto thee, into thine holy temple.*

> 74. **Hebrews 12:11-13** *Now no chastening for the present seemeth to be joyous, but grievous: nevertheless afterward it yieldeth the peaceable fruit of righteousness unto them which are exercised thereby. Wherefore lift up the hands which hang down, and the feeble knees; And make straight paths for your feet, lest that which is lame be turned out of the way; but let it rather be healed.*

Now this is exactly what happens to Israel. Let us go back to the rich man and see:

> 75. **Luke 16:23** *And in hell he lift up his eyes, being in torments, and seeth Abraham afar off, and Lazarus in his bosom.*

Many characters in the scripture lifted up their eyes to see something (Ezekiel 8:5, Daniel 8:3, Zechariah 1:18, etc.). This means that their eyes of understanding were enlightened to something that they did not previously know. Literally, they were raised to a higher level of understanding.

So what the Jewish nation will come to realize is that Jesus (Lazarus) was correct, and that they themselves, being "afar off" from Abraham are not in good standing with God. This is what the cleansing fire can do. Affliction can cause a nation to come to its senses and repent! Israel's eyes will be opened as they return to God.

SAMSON'S BLINDNESS

Samson was a literal person in the Old Testament, who was also a symbolic type of the nation of Israel. He was a Nazarite from birth. He was to be separated from the world to do only the things of God, and only as God wished. Israel was to do the same. Neither Samson nor Israel separated themselves from the things of this world. One day a lion came up against Samson.

> 76. **Judges 14:5** *Then went Samson down, and his father and his mother, to Timnath, and came to the vineyards of Timnath: and, behold, a young lion roared against him.*

This lion represents the Lion of the tribe of Judah: Jesus Christ (Revelation 5:5-6). The lion "roared" against the people of Israel. In the same way, Jesus <u>preached</u> contrary to the Jewish doctrines. Samson slew the lion in the same way that the rich man caused the death of Lazarus:

> 77. **Judges 14:6-7** *And the Spirit of the LORD came mightily upon him, and he rent him as he would have rent a kid, and he had nothing in his hand: but he told not his father or his mother what he had done. And he went down, and talked with the woman; and she pleased Samson well.*

Samson sought after strange women, which typifies Israel's unfaithfulness to God. The Israelites chased after false teachings that pleased the <u>flesh</u>, not the soul.

> 78. **Judges 14:8** *And after a time he returned to take her, and he turned aside to see the carcase of the lion: and, behold, there was a*

swarm of bees and honey in the carcase of the lion.

Jesus said it was expedient that he should go and be killed as the lion was (John 16:7), so that he could send the Comforter (the Holy Spirit).

Out of the carcass of the lion, there came forth a swarm of bees carrying honey. This signified the 120 people in the upper room (a swarm) that received the Holy Spirit because Jesus left to stand at his Father's right hand. He left so that he could send the Holy Spirit. Likewise, his followers carried forth the sweetness of the gospel. They came forth carrying that message with boldness because they were comforted, anointed, and empowered by the Comforter.

Samson had seven locks of hair on his head (Judges 16:19). <u>This represents the seven spirits of God</u> (see Isaiah 11:2, Zechariah 3:9, 4:10, Revelation 1:4, 3:1, and 4:5).

> 79. **Revelation 5:6** *And I beheld, and, lo, in the midst of the throne and of the four beasts, and in the midst of the elders, stood a Lamb as it had been slain, having seven horns and seven eyes, which are the seven Spirits of God sent forth into all the earth.*

When the seven locks on Samson's head were shaven, God's Spirit departed from him (Israel), and blindness (in part) happened to him, as it would later happen to them. Jesus said in **John 14:1** *...ye believe in God, believe also in me.* So Israel was not completely blind. They saw well enough to believe in God, but just not well enough to believe in the Messiah. They were blind, but only in part!

80. **Judges 16:19-21** *And she made him sleep upon her knees; and she called for a man, and she caused him to shave off the seven locks of his head; and she began to afflict him, and his strength went from him. And she said, The Philistines be upon thee, Samson. And he awoke out of his sleep, and said, I will go out as at other times before, and shake myself. And he wist not that <u>the LORD was departed from him</u>. But the Philistines took him, <u>and put out his eyes</u>, and brought him down to Gaza, and bound him with fetters of brass; and he did grind in the prison house.*

Grinding in the prison house speaks of the second meaning of "gnashing of teeth." The first meaning is "to mock." The second meaning is "to be in agony." God often stated in the scripture that He would "melt" people in the fires of affliction (see #37). The Hebrew meaning of the word translated "melt" denotes that they would gnash with their teeth, somewhat like the emotions that Peter had when he wept bitterly after denying the Lord.

As Israel came out of the wilderness in Moses' day, so will the church will come out of its "bewildered" state, for all to glorify the Lord <u>in</u> His saints, and for all to admire Him <u>in</u> them that believe (2 Thessalonians 1:10, Joshua 2:9-11, and 4:24).

Samson's hair grew back and his strength returned, and in the same way Israel will come back into the light (lifting up their eyes).

81. **Judges 16:22** *Howbeit the hair of his head began to grow again after he was shaven.*

THIRSTING FOR RIGHTEOUSNESS

We know that all the sins of the world were heaped on Christ's shoulders. The Bible states that he was made sin for us (2 Corinthians 5:21). When he was made sin, the sin of the world was heaped on him. Jesus said in **Matthew 5:6** *Blessed are they which do hunger and thirst after righteousness: for they shall be filled.* If we are seeking after righteousness, we will seek to rid our lives of sin and accept him as our Savior. He will help us accomplish this goal.

The torment in hell of the rich man is Israel's punishment for the rejection of Christ. The closer to God one is and the more one knows His will, the greater the punishment when one turns away from Him. Satan knew God's will and roamed anywhere but the highest places in heaven. He was cast out for a period of six thousand years to the Earth. His torment, or hell, is his distance from God. When it says of the rich man: *in hell he lift up his eyes, being in torments*, it is describing Israel's punishment for rejecting Christ. Israel has been disbanded and persecuted for almost two thousand years. This was their "hell," the place of the rich man's torments.

In regard to the "great gulf," Abraham states that one cannot pass from one side to the other. This tells us that Israel <u>must</u> endure her punishment. The judgement of God has been handed down and cannot be changed. The "great gulf" is <u>fixed</u>! The burned house may not be fully destroyed, but it was still burnt.

The final verses describe the rich man asking for one to be sent back from the dead to warn his brethren of this judgement. Abraham states that they (Israel) will need to hear and to heed Moses and the prophets. Why? Moses and the prophets spoke of Jesus long before he arrived on Earth. They spoke God's word and will. If one does not study Moses and the prophets, one will not believe even if one returned from the dead. Jesus speaking this parable foreshadowed his own death and rejection by the people of Israel. He did return from the dead and they still did not believe.

The explanation of this parable is important, not only in its true meaning, but because many churches use this scripture verse to support the concept of a "hell" after death. As we have just discovered, this parable cannot be taken literally, as parables should not be interpreted literally, and it does not support the concept of a hell after death. In fact the parable supports just the opposite; that hell can be here on earth, when we are distanced from God's word and will.

As stated previously, the dead know not anything, a state which Jesus experienced as his life began to leave his body. As his mind began to "know nothing," there was only one thing that he remembered, one thing that he would last forget, the one thing that mattered to him most of all: the fact that he had a wonderful relationship with his Father in heaven. How horrible it must have been for him to have that one last memory, and realize that this relationship was being severed. Some of the last words he spoke were: *My God, my God, why hast thou forsaken me?* He was severed from the Father by the sin placed upon him for our sakes. Always be very cautious and sure that our behavior never separates us from God. We should always thirst for righteousness. "Thirst" expresses a fervent desire.

Now let us look at Samson once again. Samson once killed a thousand men with the jawbone of an ass (Judges 15:15), and afterward he was thirsty:

> 82. **Judges 15:18-19** *And he was sore athirst, and called on the LORD, and said, Thou hast given this great deliverance into the hand of thy servant: and now shall I die for thirst, and fall into the hand of the uncircumcised? But God clave an hollow place that was in the jaw, and there came water thereout; and when he had drunk, his spirit came again, and he revived: wherefore he called the name thereof Enhakkore, which is in Lehi unto this day.*

During the flood of Noah's day the fountains of the great deep were broken up and the windows of heaven were opened. This is similar to what happens when one receives the baptism of the Holy Spirit. Speaking in tongues was a necessary sign and evidence of the baptism of the Holy Spirit. Note: this promise is unto you, and to your children, and to all that are afar off (Acts 2:39).

Jesus said that inside of you would be a well of water springing up (dayspring or utterance) into everlasting life (John 4:14 and 7:38). The spirit (The Hebrew **neshamah**) given to you at birth begins to grow and build up like a waterspout (broken open from the great deep) and the Holy Spirit (dove) descends (windows of heaven opened) and it begins to overflow (destroying all the fleshly carnal nature). A person is greatly comforted by the Holy Spirit because they supernaturally experience being in good standing with God, and their spirit is revived. Where does this comfort manifest itself from? God clave a hollow place that was in the jaw, and water came thereout. The word "clave" denotes a readiness to <u>burst</u> open or a gushing forth. This is the comfort that the rich man was asking for in this parable.

> 83. **Luke 16:24** *And he cried and said, Father Abraham, have mercy on me, and send Lazarus, that he may dip the tip of his finger in water, and cool my tongue; for I am tormented in this flame.*

Lifting up the eyes and crying out for mercy shows repentance, getting saved, and being born again. Asking for the cooling of the tongue is seeking the Holy Spirit manifested by the evidence of speaking in tongues. This takes away the <u>torment</u> of fighting our carnal nature, (or destroying the flesh) <u>on</u> <u>our own</u>. The Spirit of God gives us that rest that we should labor to enter into.

> 84. **Isaiah 28:11-12** *For with stammering lips and another tongue will he speak to this people. To whom he said, This is the rest wherewith ye may cause the weary to rest; and this is the refreshing: yet they would not hear.*

> 85. **Hebrews 4:10-11** *For he that is entered into his rest, he also hath <u>ceased from his own works</u>, as God did from his. Let us <u>labour therefore to enter into that rest</u>, lest any man fall after the same example of unbelief.*

86. **Hebrews 10:38** *Now the just shall live by faith: but if any man draw back, my soul shall have no pleasure in him.*

Note that all the suffering (affliction) this world has to offer does not compare to the suffering (torment) of knowing that God is angry with you. Being comforted by God can enrich one to endure the sufferings of life.

87. **Isaiah 48:21** *And they thirsted not when he led them through the deserts: he caused the waters to flow out of the rock for them: he clave the rock also, and the waters gushed out.*

Now back to the gloomy message from God to the people of Israel:

88. **Luke 16:25-26** *But Abraham said, Son, remember that thou in thy lifetime receivedst thy good things, and likewise Lazarus evil things: but now he is comforted, and thou art tormented. And beside all this, between us and you there is a great gulf fixed: so that they which would pass from hence to you cannot; neither can they pass to us, that would come from thence.*

COOLING THE TONGUE

There is something happening today known as the Messianic movement. In America and Canada alone, there have been three hundred thousand Jews who have now lifted up their eyes to see that Jesus is the Messiah and that Israel has been wrong. Note that this is written in the year 1994! These Jews have received the Lord Jesus Christ into their hearts. Thirty thousand (10%) of them have now received the baptism of the Holy Spirit, cooling their tongues and comforting them. They have found favor in God's eyes by not only accepting Jesus as Lord, but by also seeking the Holy Spirit to guide them as they profess that he is Lord. They are "turning aside to see the carcass of the lion," and taking of the honey as they go on (their Christian journey) eating (Judges 14:9), and cooling their tongues.

> 89. **1 Samuel 14:29** *Then said Jonathan, My father hath troubled the land: see, I pray you, how <u>mine eyes have been enlightened, because I tasted a little of this honey</u>.*

This is a major sign of the times. It shows that the gulf (or separation) between Lazarus and the rich man is practically no longer there, and the Jewish people are now crossing over as Israel's eyes are being opened, and the fullness (end) of the Gentiles (age) is about to come to a close.

> 90. **Luke 16:27-28** *Then he said, I pray thee therefore, father, that thou wouldest send him to my father's house: For I have five brethren; that he may testify unto them, lest they also come into this place of torment.*

The Apostle Peter made a statement that explains who these five brethren are.

91a. **1 Peter 1:1** *Peter, an apostle of Jesus Christ, to the strangers scattered throughout Pontus, Galatia, Cappadocia, Asia, and Bithynia,*

There was a great dispersion of the Jewish people as previously prophesied in the book of Hosea. I mentioned this earlier in relation to the Jewish nation being in hell, or swallowed up, like Jonah was to *be among the Gentiles as a vessel wherein is no pleasure* (Hosea 8:8) They have been dispersed, as Peter said; "scattered" throughout these five regions of the world.

91b. **Deuteronomy 32:20-26** *And he said, I will hide my face from them, I will see what their end shall be: for they are a very froward generation, children in whom is no faith. They have moved me to jealousy with that which is not God; they have provoked me to anger with their vanities: and I will move them to jealousy with those which are not a people; I will provoke them to anger with a foolish nation. For a fire is kindled in mine anger, and shall burn unto the lowest hell, and shall consume the earth with her increase, and set on fire the foundations of the mountains. I will heap mischiefs upon them; I will spend mine arrows upon them. They shall be burnt with hunger, and devoured with burning heat, and with bitter destruction: I will also send the teeth of beasts upon them, with the poison of serpents of the dust. The sword without, and terror within, shall destroy both the young man and the virgin, the suckling also with the man of gray hairs. I said, I would scatter them into corners, I would make the remembrance of them to cease from among men:*

The rich man wanted Lazarus to go out from the grave and give his brothers a testimony that they should not do the same as he had done. Abraham's (God's) reply to this request was this:

92. Luke 16:29 *Abraham saith unto him, They have Moses and the prophets; let them hear them.*

The Old Testament prophets foretold of Christ long before he came. Here are some verses that simply repeat what God was saying to the nation of Israel in Abraham's message; things which they were to take heed to.

93. 1 Peter 1:10-11 *Of which salvation the prophets have inquired and searched diligently, who prophesied of the grace that should come unto you: Searching what, or what manner of time the Spirit of Christ which was in them did signify, when it testified beforehand the sufferings of Christ, and the glory that should follow.*

Moses gave the Law. Whenever the Jewish people thought of the Law and the requirements of God, they thought of Moses. And whenever they thought of the prophets, they thought of Elijah. Moses and Elijah represented the Law and the prophets. They prophesied and testified beforehand about Christ, <u>by the Spirit</u> of Christ which was in them.

94: 2 Peter 2:21 *For it had been better for them not to have known the way of righteousness, than, after they have known it, to turn from the holy commandment delivered unto them.*

There was one other element in the scriptures which testified beforehand of Christ, and that was the book of Psalms. These three elements in the Old Testament scriptures were spoken of by Christ, as he indicated that they completed the task of fully revealing all one needed to know to recognize who he was.

95. **Matthew 13:33-35** *Another parable spake he unto them; The kingdom of heaven is like unto leaven, which a woman took, and hid in three measures of meal, till the whole was leavened. All these things spake Jesus unto the multitude in parables; and without a parable spake he not unto them: That it might be fulfilled which was spoken by the prophet, saying, I will open my mouth in parables; I will utter things which have been kept secret from the foundation of the world.* (see Luke 24:44)

In the above verse Jesus speaks of three measures of meal that were <u>hid</u>. He said this as he fulfilled prophesies that foretold of him uttering (or speaking) things which have been kept secret from the foundation of the world. These things were hidden in the Old Testament.

God freely gave us salvation. This salvation is ministered to us supernaturally as He applies His grace to our hearts and we change. We never sought Him, He sought us (Romans 3:11 and John 6:44). Yet there are things that we are supposed to seek after. It is like digging for gold. We search for hope in Christ after we have been drawn to him.

96. **John 5:39** *Search the scriptures; for in them ye think ye have eternal life: and they are they which testify of me.*

Here is another place which speaks of the fact that these elements in the Old Testament spoke of Christ and his sufferings beforehand, only most people never think of these verses in this light:

> 97. **Matthew 17:1-3** *And after six days Jesus taketh Peter, James, and John his brother, and bringeth them up into an high mountain apart, And was transfigured before them: and his face did shine as the sun, and his raiment was white as the light. And, behold, there appeared unto them Moses and Elias talking with him.... And as they came down from the mountain, Jesus charged them, saying, Tell the vision to no man, until the Son of man be risen again from the dead.*

> 98a. **Luke 9:30-31** *And, behold, there talked with him two men, which were Moses and Elias: Who appeared in glory, and spake of his decease which he should accomplish at Jerusalem.*

Notice that the Spirit of God stated through Matthew that *there appeared* unto them...Moses and Elias talking with him. Christ later called what they saw a vision. God gives people revelations through visions and dreams, which are called *visions of the night* (Job 4:13). God said of the future that *...your old men shall dream dreams, your young men shall see visions* (Joel 2:28).

Consider this for a moment. Nebuchadnezzar, king of Babylon, saw a great image in a dream, also referred to as a vision in his head upon his bed (Daniel 2:28). This great image (Daniel 2:31) was <u>not actually there</u> physically or spiritually. It was something that he saw in his mind from God which revealed a certain truth.

81

The same applies to the mount of transfiguration. These men saw a vision, something that appeared unto them. Moses and Elijah were not there either physically, nor were their spirits present. According to the whole tenor of what the Bible teaches, Moses and Elias are yet resting in peace unto this very day, knowing nothing…, waiting until their "change comes" (see #11) in the day of their resurrection.

> 98b. **Ecclesiastes 9:5-6** *For the living know that they shall die: but the dead know not any thing, neither have they any more a reward; for the memory of them is forgotten. Also their love, and their hatred, and their envy, is now perished; neither have they any more a portion for ever in any thing that is done under the sun.*

The purpose of what was revealed to them in this vision was to verify that the Law and the prophets, two of the three elements in the Old Testament scriptures, *testified beforehand the sufferings of Christ, and the glory that should follow.* (1 Peter 1:11)

So what Abraham (or God) told the nation of Israel is that they should search the scriptures for they (the scriptures) are they (the prophets of old) which testified of him, and that they should hear them. That is to say that they should understand what those prophets stated pertaining to Christ and apply those scriptures to their lives through obedience to them, instead of ignoring them.

The rich man asked for something else! Imagine that! Abraham (God) gave Israel the key to salvation but they refused it.

> 99. **Luke 16:30** *And he said, Nay, father Abraham: but if one went unto them from the dead, they will repent.*

This is what the rich man felt he needed; Lazarus, this person who was found to be in favor with God, to return from the dead. God responds by telling him that his fellow brethren (the Israelites) would still be too stubborn to believe, even if he received what he felt his brethren needed.

Acceptance of Christ's resurrection is the door to their hell being opened, but they did not understand the key to open it. Abraham said the key was written in the Old Testament scriptures. If you do not turn the key, or accept what is written concerning Jesus, then the door will not open, or you will never therefore accept him. This is how he stated it:

> 100. **Luke 16:31** *And he said unto him, If they hear not Moses and the prophets, neither will they be persuaded, though one rose from the dead.*

If they missed the points the prophets made about a resurrection, then they would not believe it if it actually happened. This is how the prophet David prophesied this concerning Christ:

> 101. **Psalms 16:10** *For thou wilt not leave my soul in hell; neither wilt thou suffer thine Holy One to see corruption.*

If they only had respected David's statement concerning Christ going to the grave (hell) and not being left there to rot, then they might have accepted Christ as the Messiah, the Holy One. Samson was also a prophet that stated through a riddle that salvation (sweetness) would come from the Lion. Israel will take up to the third thousand year period to figure this out.

102. **Judges 14:14** *And he* (Samson) *said unto them, Out of the eater came forth meat* (as Jesus said, *my flesh is meat indeed*), *and out of the strong came forth sweetness. And* <u>*they could not in three days*</u> *expound the riddle.*

EXPECT THE UNEXPECTED WHEN SINNING

Jesus healed a certain centurion's servant one day because of the man's faith in him. Jesus stated that the man, who was a Gentile, had this faith in Christ's authority because of <u>his obedience</u> to the authority of the Father. Here is what he said:

103. **Matthew 8:9-12** *For I am a man <u>under authority</u>, having soldiers under me: and I say to this man, Go, and he goeth; and to another, Come, and he cometh; and to my servant, Do this, and he doeth it. When Jesus heard it, he marvelled, and said to them that followed, Verily I say unto you, I have not found so great faith, no, <u>not in Israel</u>. And I say unto you, That many shall come from the east and west, and shall sit down with Abraham, and Isaac, and Jacob, in the kingdom of heaven. But the children of the kingdom shall be cast out into outer darkness: there shall be weeping and gnashing of teeth.*

Jesus states that many from the east and the west, which would encompass all Gentile nations, would sit down (perhaps to eat or sup) with the patriarchs of Israel in the house (hold) of faith. The "fathers" were considered to be "in the kingdom of heaven" because of their faith. To sit down with them in that kingdom signified that the Gentiles would enter into God's grace and be saved, and eat, or (as it were) to learn of God as their souls are nourished unto eternal life.

The children of the kingdom, who were the Jews by birthright, were going to be cast out, or no longer in God's favor like the rich man standing "afar off." To be cast into outer darkness signified that there would be no hope for them as a nation, and that they would stay in complete ignorance, totally devoid of any light whatsoever. Jesus said, *I am the light of the world...* (John 8:12). Therefore these people would not only be ignorant of any knowledge pertaining to him, but they would be devoid of him and the salvation that comes through him. This would cause a continuous lack of peace; weeping and gnashing of teeth. Jesus later told them of this condemnation upon Israel:

> 104. **Luke 20:13-16** *Then said the lord of the vineyard, What shall I do? I will send my beloved son: it may be they will reverence him when they see him. But when the husbandmen saw him, they reasoned among themselves, saying, This is the heir: come, let us kill him, that the inheritance may be ours. So they cast him out of the vineyard, and killed him. What therefore shall the lord of the vineyard do unto them? He shall come and destroy these husbandmen, and shall give the vineyard to others. And when they heard it, they said, God forbid.*

The nation of Israel killed God's Son, Jesus Christ. When Jesus rebuked them for their unbelief, he told them the Father would bring destruction upon them and that the Father would then bring His favor upon "others," referring to a people other than the Jews. The Jewish people understood the depth of what he had said but they did not figure that God would do such a thing. Being in their sin, they should have expected the unexpected. God turned His back on the Jews and turned toward the Gentiles.

IN WRATH REMEMBER MERCY

As I mentioned earlier, a house burning is comparable to a person being in hell, or suffering (reaping) the consequences of what they have sown. That house can burn until it is put out, signifying repentance; or it can burn to the ground; where one is consumed in their iniquity (Genesis 19:15) by any means of punishment that God may choose. This punishment, in either case, rids the universe of sin and will come to an end through repentance, or because there will be nothing else to consume. They will be consumed in God's wrath until they burn "no more." Remember, being spoken out of existence is a punishment that lasts forever.

The sacrifices of the Old Testament were to last forever, but there was a change that occurred (see Hebrews 7:12). The word "forever" must be understood to mean forever <u>until a change comes</u>. That change is the quenching of the burning house (repentance), or until it can burn no more (a condition of non-existence). Who is the only one that can rebuild a burnt house with only pieces left to work with? A Jewish carpenter of course!

Many people reject God because they do not see this merciful side of Him. Satan does not want people to see Him as a God of love, but as a God of overbearing vengeance. Satan desires that people shake their fists at heaven for reasons (or lies) that <u>Satan</u> gave them. The Bible may <u>appear</u> to say that hell is a place where souls go to fry throughout eternity, but it does not! Any false doctrine must <u>appear</u> to be true. It can only appear to be true when someone twists certain scriptures through wrong interpretation and by causing other scriptures to be ignored. One thing I have found is that deceivers prey on the weak, depending upon one's ignorance of the scriptures. It has been my hope that I could give enough scriptural proof to verify that if one dies without repentance and acceptance of the Savior Jesus Christ, they will not have eternal life, period. Viewing life eternal in a place of punishing is not scriptural. Some people know the concept of Hades derives from a pagan religion (Greek mythology). The doctrine itself comes from a myth. People fear God for the wrong reason!

> 105. **Isaiah 29:13** *Wherefore the Lord said, Forasmuch as this people draw near me with their mouth, and with their lips do honour me, but have removed their heart far from me, and their fear toward me is taught by the precept of men:*

Now, if people fear God for the wrong reason, it may be that they are serving Him for the wrong reason, i.e. self preservation. Jesus preserves! Fire and brimstone preaching has been practiced for a long time. A preacher learns it from his teachers, and it is passed down to others through tradition.

The problem with "fire and brimstone" preaching is:

1) It is based on wrong interpretations of the scripture which simply is not true. The term "lies" in Hebrew is the same word for "idols." We cannot teach lies.

2) Although it is not true, it appears to be effective. Preachers therefore may continue preaching what is false.

People that hear messages of God's wrath are looking mostly at a punishment. "Fire and brimstone" preaching <u>pushes</u> people into God's arms through <u>fear</u>. God does not want people pushed into His arms through fear or by any other means. The Bible says that God <u>draws us</u> to His Son. This means we are <u>pulled</u>, not pushed!

> 106. **John 6:44** *No man can come to me, except the Father which hath sent me draw him: and I will raise him up at the last day.*

> 107. **John 6:65** *And he said, Therefore said I unto you, that no man can come unto me, except it were given unto him of my Father.*

Many people that stood by when Jesus said this were there for the wrong reason. Had they been there for the right reason, they probably would not have stood up and walked out on him.

> 108. **John 6:66** *From that time <u>many</u> of his disciples went back, and walked no more with him.*

Pastors beware! Ye that place food on the tables to feed His flocks. If one is chased into God's arms by reason of fear or self-preservation, they will be chased <u>out</u> of His arms for cause of fear. Please allow me to illustrate my point. Persecution comes and a person has a knife placed against their throat because of their testimony that they hold and preach. Self-preservation will persist if they had not met the God of love, but the God of vengeance. They may <u>not</u> have met God for who He <u>really</u> is. He draws us through His love, not pushing us through fear.

109. **1 John 4:18-19** *There is no fear in love; but perfect love casteth out fear: because fear hath torment. He that feareth is not made perfect in love. We love him, because he first loved us.*

We see impending death before us because of our sins. We learn that because of impending death, God has offered us an alternative; life through His Son Jesus Christ, who died on the cross for us. When we realize that He first seeks us, it causes us to seek Him. If we have found the God that loves us, pulled in by His love, then nothing will pull us out of His arms.

110. **Romans 8:38-39** *For I am persuaded, that neither death, nor life, nor angels, nor principalities, nor powers, nor things present, nor things to come, Nor height, nor depth, nor any other creature, shall be able to separate us from the <u>love</u> of God, which is in Christ Jesus our Lord.*

Most people do not know the truth simply because it was never shown to them, or not shown <u>properly</u>. It has never been pointed out to them. They read the words..."shall not see life," and unless they were told, they blink their eyes and miss the point. Once led to the truth, it is as obvious as night and day. One can begin to see this truth everywhere in scripture. **Romans 6:23** *For the wages of sin is death; but the gift of God is eternal life through Jesus Christ our Lord.*

Satan wants people to be bound by his lies. He does not want them to meet God for who He really is. He wants people to believe that God is an unmerciful tyrant. He knows that countless millions have, and will yet reject God because the only view they get of God is Satan's point of view when speaking of punishment. God only chastens us for our own sakes. A proper view of the punishments of God and the motives behind them allows us to see Him as the God of <u>love</u>.

Unfortunately, many will not see that. The <u>traditional</u> view is the mainstream view, and it is the few that are saved, *for wide is the gate, and broad is the way that leadeth to destruction, and many shall seek to enter in, and shall not be able* (Luke 13:24). The mainstream view is within the number of man, and those that adhere to it within their minds (or foreheads) are marked, for they accept (or receive) man's ways, not God's. Those that come to understand pure doctrine (Daniel 11:33) will have to contradict many things that are traditionally taught. Some are not marked in the mind, for they know the truth, but they will be marked in the right hand of fellowship by going along with the lie, and refusing to "go against the flow."[11] Hopefully, we will always know and act in accordance with God's truth and will. As this world comes to its wicked end, we <u>must</u> reveal God for who His Word truly reveals Him to be.

111. **Isaiah 28:7-10** *But they also have erred through wine, and through strong drink* (deception) *are out of the way; the priest and the prophet have erred through strong drink, they are swallowed up of wine, they are out of the way through strong drink; they err in vision, they stumble in judgment. For all tables are full of vomit and filthiness, so that there is no place clean. Whom shall he teach knowledge? and whom shall he make to understand*

---

[11] This is what is meant by not kissing the mouth of Baal (becoming so intimate with false religion that it penetrates into your mind), and by not bowing the knee to Baal (serving under or fellowshipping a system of false religion in spite of your understanding of its evils). See 1 Kings 19:18.

doctrine? them that are weaned from the milk, and drawn from the breasts. For precept must be upon precept, precept upon precept; line upon line, line upon line; here a little, and there a little:

RESURRECTION OF THE DEAD

In closing the subject on hell, I must touch upon the doctrine of the resurrection of the dead, to establish the fact that the wicked are not a part of the first or second resurrections, thus securing that they will exist no more.

I will not go to great lengths to prove points in this area because it is another subject altogether. My goal is to keep this exposition on "hell" as short as possible for easier understanding. I will though, have to touch on the main points of this doctrine to uphold the points shown concerning hell.

As stated earlier, hell, or the grave, has a magnetic, almost demanding effect for souls. A study on the word "hell" will reveal this. Satan has the power of death (Hebrews 2:14), but Jesus came to destroy him. Satan, or death, holds its power over those that never accepted Christ, but the saved <u>will</u> come out of the grave. We are <u>saved</u> from the wages of sin, which <u>is</u> death, when we accept Christ as Lord and Savior (Romans 6:23). This is what Jesus was saying when he told Peter the following about his church:

> 112. **Matthew 16:18** *And I say also unto thee, That thou art Peter, and upon this rock I will build my church; and the gates of hell shall not prevail against it.*

Christ's people will rise! The power of the grave will lose its hold on Christ's church. The grave has to give up the dead that are his sheep. They hear his voice; for *they that hear* shall live (John 5:25). The demanding power of the grave cannot prevail over his people. They are to be saved from death. *It is finished* (John 19:30) means the wages are "paid in full" (see Matthew 18:27).

THE THIEF ON THE CROSS

The thief on the cross accepted Jesus when he called him "Lord" (Luke 23:42). He confessed his sins when he stated that he and the other thief received due reward for their deeds (Luke 23:41). He believed in the righteousness and integrity of Christ when he stated that *this man hath done nothing amiss*. He asked to be saved when he requested that Jesus "remember" him when Jesus came into His kingdom (Luke 23:42). The man did all the required things necessary in the plan of salvation; therefore he was promised that he would be saved from death.

113. **Luke 23:43** *And Jesus said unto him, Verily I say unto thee, To day shalt thou be with me in paradise.*

I must point out that the Greek language had no punctuation marks. Therefore the people that interpreted the Bible placed the comma in the place where they felt it was needed according to their understanding of the scriptures. Note that I am not saying that the Bible is wrong, nor am I discrediting a single word in it. What I am saying (despite all possible repercussions) is that there are many that feel that the comma should have been placed after the word "today" rather than before it. The proper placement of the comma will allow an understanding of that verse that stays within the whole tenor of the Bible.

When the comma falls after the word, the meaning of the verse follows along with what the entire Bible teaches; precept upon precept and line upon line, that there has not yet been a resurrection (2 Timothy 2:18), and that those that sleep in the grave (*sheol*) must wait to rise until the heavens be no more.

95

Therefore the proper way this is to be understood is: *Verily I say unto thee to day, shalt thou be with me in paradise.*

Most know that Jesus was <u>not</u> in paradise that same day, for he was yet to be in the grave (***sheol/hades***) for three days. As stated earlier, Abraham's bosom is not paradise. Jesus told John in the book of Revelation, approximately sixty years later, that people <u>will</u> (future) eat of the tree of <u>life</u> which is in the midst of the paradise of God (Revelation 2:7). Nowhere in the scriptures does it teach that Abraham's bosom is paradise! So Jesus would not have told the repentant thief that he would be there on that particular day.

This was a promise made by Christ to the repentant thief; <u>that he would be saved</u> from the death he was currently facing on <u>that</u> day. A better translation might be: "I promise you <u>this very day</u>, in this very moment, despite the very death that is staring you in the face as we speak; I <u>guarantee</u> that you will be with me in paradise."

> 114. **Revelation 2:7** *He that hath an ear, let him hear what the Spirit saith unto the churches; To him that overcometh will I give to eat of the tree of life, which is in the midst of the paradise of God.*

Jesus made this promise to be fulfilled <u>later</u>, to overcomers. Paul also made a statement that paradise was upward, not downward in hell, or the "holding place of the saints," as some actually teach.

115. **2 Corinthians 12:3-4** *And I knew such a man, (whether in the body, or out of the body, I cannot tell: God knoweth;) How that he was caught up into paradise, and heard unspeakable words, which it is not lawful for a man to utter.*

So Jesus' promise to the thief was <u>not</u> fulfilled that day, but rather, was <u>a promise made that day</u>. He would be in paradise in his time that was appointed (Job 14:13).

RESURRECTION OF THE JUST AND THE UNJUST

Paul made a statement pertaining to his beliefs before Festus, claiming that the Law and the Prophets showed that there would be a resurrection of the dead for two different classes of people. Let us take a look.

> 116. **Acts 24:14-15** *But this I confess unto thee, that after the way which they call heresy, so worship I the God of my fathers, believing all things which are written in the law and in the prophets: And have hope toward God, which they themselves also allow, that there shall be a resurrection of the dead, both of the just and unjust.*

So now we begin to consider: who are the just and who are the unjust? Let us look once again at David's statement about the three classes:

> 117a. **Psalms 1:5** *Therefore the ungodly shall not stand in the judgment, nor sinners in the congregation of the righteous.*

Notice that the word "nor" separates the ungodly from the class "sinners". We see all three classes mentioned here:

Ungodly = Wicked
Sinners = Unjust
Righteous = Just

> 117b. **1 Peter 4:18** *And if the righteous scarcely be saved, where shall the ungodly and the sinner appear?*

Once again we see that the wicked do <u>not</u> stand (rise) in the judgement. We will soon look at what is meant by the statement that the sinners do not stand in the congregation of the righteous. Note also that this verse did <u>not</u> say that the sinners would not stand in the <u>judgement</u>. They are saved, yet sinners. Paul said they <u>will</u>, but sinners do not stand in (or rise with) the congregation of the righteous. It is the ungodly that will not stand in the judgment. The wicked do not see life. The wrath of God (death) <u>abideth</u> on them (see #21).

Did not Paul say that we <u>all</u> shall stand before the judgement seat of Christ? (Romans 14:10-13). Paul was speaking to brethren, believers, the saved. There are often statements in the Bible which speak of "all" which only applies to <u>all believers</u>.

This is where the doctrine of the resurrection of the dead may seem complicated. If you thought that the wicked would rise, which most feel is what the second resurrection is all about, then you will want to carefully consider <u>each</u> point that follows. Let us start with the first resurrection.

THE RESURRECTION OF THE JUST

The word "just" means righteous or holy. It denotes equality in balance or scale, proper measure, proper judgment, or justice.

118. **Isaiah 26:7-8** *The way of the just is uprightness: thou, most upright, dost <u>weigh</u> the path of the just. Yea, in the way of thy judgments, O LORD, have we waited for thee; the desire of our soul is to thy name, and to the remembrance of thee.*

The people of the first resurrection are a <u>holy</u> people. We must seek to be holy if we are to attain to this resurrection (Philippians 3:11-14). Those who attain to the first resurrection will have the privilege to rule with Christ for a thousand years.

119. **Revelation 20:4-6** *And I saw thrones, and they sat upon them, and judgment was given unto them: and I saw the souls of them that were beheaded for the witness of Jesus, and for the word of God, and which had not worshipped the beast, neither his image, neither had received his mark upon their foreheads, or in their hands; and they lived and reigned with Christ a thousand years. But the rest of the dead lived not again until the thousand years were finished. This is the first resurrection. Blessed and holy is he that hath part in the first resurrection: on such the second death hath no power, but they shall be priests of God and of Christ, and shall reign with him a thousand years.*

To be beheaded for the witness of Christ could mean a literal death, a beheading, or a spiritual "dying to self," with no life of their own, living <u>only</u> for Christ. These are considered to be the firstfruits, for they are of the first resurrection, only 144,000.

120. **Revelation 14:1-5** *And I looked, and, lo, a Lamb stood on the mount Sion, and with him <u>an hundred forty and four thousand</u>, having his Father's name written in their foreheads. And I heard a voice from heaven, as the voice of many waters, and as the voice of a great thunder: and I heard the voice of harpers harping with their harps: And they sung as it were a new song before the throne, and before the four beasts, and the elders: and no man could learn that song but the hundred and forty and four thousand, which were redeemed from the earth. These are they which were not defiled with women; for they are virgins. These are they which follow the Lamb whithersoever he goeth. These were redeemed from among men, being the firstfruits unto God and to the Lamb. And in their mouth was found no guile: for they are without fault before the throne of God.*

They are without fault before the throne of God.

121. **2 Peter 3:14** *Wherefore, beloved, seeing that ye look for such things, be diligent that ye may be found of him in peace, without spot, and blameless.*

122. **1 Corinthians 15:20-23** *But now is Christ risen from the dead, and become the firstfruits of them that slept. For since by man came death, by man came also the resurrection of the dead. For as in Adam all die, even so in Christ shall all be made alive. But every man in his own order: Christ the firstfruits; afterward they that are Christ's at his coming.*

123. **Revelation 20:5-6** *But the rest of the dead lived not again until the thousand years were finished. This is the first resurrection. Blessed and holy is he that hath part in the first*

resurrection: on such the second death hath no power, but they shall be priests of God and of Christ, and shall reign with him a thousand years.

Notice that the above verse says that the second death has no power over them. Why? They are holy. They "pressed" to remove all sin out of their lives. The second death cannot overcome them because they overcame sin, the wages of which is death. Jesus saves us from the first death through accepting him by faith, but we must purge sin out of our lives with his constant help. You must overcome sin or you will not be raised in the first resurrection, but in the <u>second</u> resurrection. Those who do <u>not</u> overcome sin <u>after</u> their resurrection will die the second death, yet this time it will be a permanent death.

124. **Revelation 2:11** *He that hath an ear, let him hear what the Spirit saith unto the churches; He that overcometh shall not be hurt of the second death.*

Notice the promises to overcomers found in the book of Revelation:

1) Eat of the tree of life (Revelation 2:7)
2) Shall not be hurt of the second death (guarantee on life eternal (Revelation 2:11)
3) Eat of the hidden manna and receive a white stone with a <u>new name written on it</u> (Revelation 2:17)
4) Power over the nations to rule them with a rod of iron (Revelation 2:26)
5) Clothed in white raiment, and their names <u>not</u> blotted out of the book of life (Revelation 3:5)

6. <u>The name of God</u>, the name of the city of God, and <u>my new name</u> written upon him (Revelation 3:12)

7. Granted to sit with Christ in His throne (Revelation 3:21)

These things are promised to <u>overcomers</u>. These promises <u>match</u> the statements made pertaining to the 144,000 first fruits with the Father's name written in their foreheads: those that will rule with Christ. These overcomers have <u>his</u> new name, meaning that they are his Bride.

> 125a. **Revelation 21:2** *And I John saw <u>the holy city</u>, new Jerusalem, <u>coming down</u> from God out of heaven, <u>prepared as a bride adorned for her husband</u>.*

> 125b. **Revelation 21:9-10** *And there came unto me one of the seven angels which had the seven vials full of the seven last plagues, and talked with me, saying, Come hither, <u>I will shew thee the bride</u>, the Lamb's wife. And he carried me away in the spirit to a great and high mountain, and <u>shewed me that great city</u>, <u>the holy Jerusalem, descending out of heaven from God</u>,*

That great mountain is Mount Zion, the Bride, <u>on</u> which the Lamb stood (rules over). There are only 144,000 members of the first resurrection: 144,000 just people or justices.

> 126. **Hebrews 12:22-23** *But ye are come unto mount Sion, and unto the city of the living God, the heavenly Jerusalem, and to an innumerable company of angels, To the general assembly and church of the firstborn, which are written in heaven, and to God the Judge of all, and to the spirits of just men made perfect,*

The second resurrection is not for the ungodly. They are not raised to be cast back into death. The ungodly are dead already. The wrath of God (death) <u>abideth</u> on them. Why pull them from the grave to put them back? Death prevails! It has its victory over those who never gave the victory to God. God would not raise them to tell them what they missed out on. There would be no purpose in it. This would be spiteful. The second resurrection is for the saved who had not completely cleansed <u>themselves</u> from all unrighteousness.

The Just press for the high calling until they attain perfection, with the help of Christ. The Just shall live by faith.

127. **Romans 9:30-31** *What shall we say then? That the Gentiles, which followed not after righteousness, have attained to righteousness, even the righteousness which is of faith. But Israel, which followed after the law of righteousness, hath not attained to the law of righteousness.*

128. **Hebrews 7:19** *For the law made nothing perfect, but the bringing in of a better hope did; by the which we draw nigh unto God.*

After having understood the first principles of faith, and all other doctrines, we should go on to press for perfection.

129. **Hebrews 6:1-3** *Therefore leaving the principles of the doctrine of Christ, let us go on unto perfection; not laying again the foundation of repentance from dead works, and of faith toward God, Of the doctrine of baptisms, and of laying on of hands, and of resurrection of the dead, and of eternal judgment. And this will we*

do, if God permit.

130. **Hebrews 6:18-20** *That by two immutable things, in which it was impossible for God to lie, we might have a strong consolation, who have fled for refuge to lay hold upon the hope set before us: Which hope we have as an anchor of the soul, both sure and stedfast, and which entereth into that within the veil; Whither the forerunner is for us entered, even Jesus, made an high priest for ever after the order of Melchisedec.*

JUDGED ACCORDING TO OUR WORKS

Baptism gives us a good conscience toward God, but it does not put away the filth of the flesh, our carnal nature (1 Peter 3:21). <u>We</u> must do that. We must clean up our sins, with the help of our Lord, but it is something He expects <u>us</u> to do.

131. **Philippians 2:12** *Wherefore, my beloved, as ye have always obeyed, not as in my presence only, but now much more in my absence, <u>work out your own</u> salvation with fear and trembling.*

132. **James 2:22-24** *Seest thou how faith wrought with his works, and by works was faith made perfect? And the scripture was fulfilled which saith, Abraham believed God, and it was imputed unto him for righteousness: and he was called the Friend of God. Ye see then how that by works a man is justified, and not by faith only.*

This shows that we <u>must</u> get sin out of our lives, for we will be judged according to our works. The following are some verses that prove this point:

133. **Revelation 20:12** *And I saw the dead, small and great* (peasants <u>and</u> kings), *stand before God; and the books were opened: and another book was opened, which is the book of life: and the dead were judged out of those things which were written in the books, according to their <u>works</u>.*

134. **Revelation 14:13** *And I heard a voice from heaven saying unto me, Write, Blessed are the dead which die in the Lord from henceforth: Yea, saith the Spirit, that they may rest from their*

labours; and their works do follow them.

135. **Proverbs 24:12** *If thou sayest, Behold, we knew it not; doth not he that pondereth the heart consider it? and he that keepeth thy soul, doth not he know it? and shall not he render to every man according to his works?*

136. **Jeremiah 32:19** *Great in counsel, and mighty in work: for thine eyes are open upon all the ways of the sons of men: to give every one according to his ways, and according to the fruit of his doings:*

137. **Matthew 16:27** *For the Son of man shall come in the glory of his Father with his angels; and then he shall reward every man according to his works.*

138. **Romans 2:6** *Who will render to every man according to his deeds:*

139. **1 Peter 1:15-22** *But as he which hath called you is holy, so be ye holy in all manner of conversation; Because it is written, Be ye holy; for I am holy. And if ye call on the Father, who without respect of persons judgeth according to every man's work, pass the time of your sojourning here in fear: Forasmuch as ye know that ye were not redeemed with corruptible things, as silver and gold, from your vain conversation received by tradition from your fathers; But with the precious blood of Christ, as of a lamb without blemish and without spot: Who verily was foreordained before the foundation of the world, but was manifest in these last times for you, Who by him do believe in God, that raised him up from the dead, and gave him glory; that your faith and hope might be in God. Seeing ye have*

purified your souls in obeying the truth through the Spirit unto unfeigned love of the brethren, see that ye love one another with a pure heart fervently:

140. **2 Timothy 3:16-17** *All scripture is given by inspiration of God, and is profitable for doctrine, for reproof, for correction, for instruction in righteousness: That the man of God may be perfect, throughly furnished unto all good works.*

We were <u>told</u> (commanded, not asked, nor given a suggestion) to *Be ye therefore perfect.* Jesus even said to what degree we were to be perfect: even as (or equal to) his Father in heaven. "Even as" signifies not less than, nor greater than, but equal to the degree that my Father in heaven is perfect (holy). Be <u>that</u> perfect!

141. **Matthew 5:48** *Be ye therefore perfect, even as your Father which is in heaven is perfect.*

Paul said that <u>he</u> pressed for the high calling, to <u>attain</u> perfection. This is that resurrection that he wanted to press for. Something attained is not what is imputed!

142. **Philippians 3:11-14** *If by any means I might attain unto the resurrection of the dead. Not as though I had already attained* (at least not yet), *either were already perfect: but I follow after, if that I may apprehend that for which also I am apprehended of Christ Jesus. Brethren, I count not myself to have apprehended: but this one thing I do, forgetting those things which are behind, and reaching forth unto those things which are before, I press toward the mark for the prize of <u>the high calling</u> of God in Christ Jesus.*

He later said that he had that attained the crown of life: something only the Bride (the 144,000) was promised.

143. **2 Timothy 4:6-8** *For <u>I am now ready</u> to be offered, and the time of my departure is at hand. <u>I have fought</u> a good fight, I have <u>finished</u> my course, I have <u>kept</u> the faith: Henceforth there is laid up for me a crown of righteousness, which the Lord, the righteous judge, shall give me <u>at that day</u>: and not to me only, but unto all them also that love his appearing.*

144. **Revelation 19:7-8** *Let us be glad and rejoice, and give honour to him: for the marriage of the Lamb is come, and <u>his wife hath made herself ready</u>. And to her was granted that she should be arrayed in fine linen, clean and white: for <u>the fine linen is the righteousness of saints</u>.*

<u>Overcomers</u> enter into eternal life because they push sin out of their life with the help of Christ, the forerunner.

145. **1 John 2:17** *And the world passeth away, and the lust thereof: but he that doeth the will of God abideth for ever.*

146. **Ezekiel 20:11** *And I gave them my statutes, and shewed them my judgments, which if a man do, he shall even live in them.*

147. **Revelation 22:14** *Blessed are <u>they that do his commandments</u>, that <u>they may have right to the tree of life</u>, and may <u>enter in</u> through the gates into the city.*

148. **Proverbs 11:4** *Riches profit not in the day of wrath: but righteousness delivereth from death.*

149. Proverbs 16:17 *The <u>highway</u> of the upright is to depart from evil: he that keepeth his way preserveth his soul.*

Notice the word "highway." We will discuss that word and precept later.

150. 1 Timothy 6:12-14 *<u>Fight the good fight of faith, lay hold on eternal life</u>, whereunto thou art also called, and hast professed a good profession before many witnesses. I give thee charge in the sight of God, who quickeneth all things, and before Christ Jesus, who before Pontius Pilate witnessed a good confession; That thou <u>keep this commandment</u> without spot, unrebukeable, until the appearing of our Lord Jesus Christ:*

Only those that do his commandments may enter in through the gates of the city.

151. Revelation 21:27 *And there shall in no wise enter into it any thing that defileth, neither whatsoever worketh abomination, or maketh a lie: but they which are written in the Lamb's book of life.*

The first fruits are the first to enter in through the gates, having the <u>right</u> to the tree of life. This is seen in Old Testament type:

152. Exodus 23:19 *The first of the firstfruits of thy land thou shalt bring into the house of the LORD thy God. Thou shalt not seethe a kid in his mother's milk.*

It is the just that will be seen coming out of their graves first to be joined with those that are "alive and remain" (1 Thes. 4:13). That will be the first resurrection of the dead to be with the

Lord in heaven. They will <u>return</u> with Christ (see Revelation 14:1, #125 and #126) when he comes to set foot on the earth. Remember that the rest of the dead lived not again until the thousand years were finished. The just are the only ones that can judge people. No one else will have removed sin out of their lives, so how could they judge? For this very reason sinners will not stand in the congregation of the righteous. The thief on the cross shall see life, but cannot enter into eternal life until he <u>overcomes</u> his tendency to take what does not belong to him. He must yet overcome. The Bride has already overcome before death, they have made themselves ready to be like Jesus (righteous). The thief never earned the right to rule because he had no time to make himself ready (to be internally or spiritually fit).

153. **1 John 3:2** *Beloved, now are we the sons of God, and it doth not yet appear what we shall be: but we know that, when he shall appear, we shall be like him; for we shall see him as he is.*

John was saying: "we are sons, but not as we want to be; but we <u>will</u> be in the day that Jesus comes." The word "like" signifies same in appearance and character.

THE RESURRECTION OF THE UNJUST
Sin After The Resurrection?

This is the multitude without number. It will consist of all the people that obeyed God according to His guidelines in the dispensation in which they lived. In that obedience, they were saved from death, but they will still have the second death to overcome. The multitude will stand before the Just, at the great white throne judgment.

> 154a. **Revelation 20:11** *And I saw a great white throne, and him that sat on it, from whose face the earth and the heaven fled away; and there was found no place for them.*

Christ rules over that throne: The Just.

> 154b. **John 5:30** *I can of mine own self do nothing: as I hear, I judge: and my judgment is just; because I seek not mine own will, but the will of the Father which hath sent me.*

The Bible states that Satan will be bound for a thousand years. At the point of his binding, the chain about his neck will be shortened to nothing. He will not be able to have any activity whatsoever. I liken it to being placed in a box for a thousand years without any outside influence coming in, and none going out. He will have nothing to do but think, in what is like solitary confinement. He will be alone with his thoughts with nothing to take his mind off his troubles for a thousand years. It will be quite maddening.

During this time, the earth will be repopulated similar to what occurred after Noah's flood. The Bride of Christ will be reigning over those still alive on the earth. Since sin is inherited, each generation will need help to overcome sin, to remove it out of their lives. The Bride will be helping them to accomplish this task.

There will be no blind justice then, but perfect judgement. Just as each generation became progressively worse since the Garden of Eden, during the Millennial Reign each generation will become progressively better under this perfect judgement and perfect government. This will take one thousand years to complete.

There will also be another group of 144,000 which will join the original group in their efforts to help all others overcome. This second group is actually seen earlier on in Revelation 7. They are part of the restored Jewish people (see Revelation 17:4-8). These Jews will have the seal of God in their foreheads. The first group was virgins (Revelation 14:3-4) which were redeemed from the earth (not just Israel), having His name written in their foreheads. You will see these two groups with a total sum of 288,000, in type in 1 Chronicles 27, and 288 captains in type in 1 Chronicles 25.

After the thousand years are finished, all those who are saved, but have not yet perfected themselves, will rise again. Satan will be loosed to deceive once more. He will be enabled, through them, to stir up more trouble. Another outbreak of sin will follow as Satan gathers those that he can to battle against the Lord in the last and final battle (which occurs at the end of the

1000 years after Armageddon).

> 155. **Revelation 20:7-8** *And when the thousand years are expired, Satan shall be loosed out of his prison, And shall go out to deceive the nations which are in the four quarters of the earth, Gog and Magog, to gather them together to battle: the number of whom is as the sand of the sea.*

God will raise up each person according to their generations. Daniel was told when he would rise:

> 156. **Daniel 12:13** *But go thou thy way till the end be: for thou shalt rest, and stand <u>in thy lot at the end of the days</u>.*

The people of Abraham's day would be totally shocked to be raised up on the very same day as people of <u>this</u> day and age. For example: to say "no" to one's parents was considered a high crime in Abraham's day, but today children slay their parents. To be raised on the very same day would be chaotic, so each generation is raised according to their <u>lot</u>.

Abraham, and those of his lot, will get to meet Christ as their Savior. The Old Testament people who are raised are raised because they met <u>those</u> requirements set down by God during the dispensation in which they lived. As they meet Christ as the pattern of perfection, those of the second resurrection will learn to be like him as <u>they</u> overcome. Remember that the Law made nothing (or nobody) perfect, so all the Old Testament saints will need this. They will also learn of his immeasurable mercy as they watch the next, and <u>worse</u>, lots raised to overcome.

Understand that this is not a second chance. Old Testament people have a chance and will be raised because they made the right choice in obeying God as He required in their day. All people during the time of Grace were given a chance and will be raised because they made the correct choice in accepting Jesus Christ, as was required of them. This is not a chance to be saved from death, for each have already chosen life. This will be the time to overcome (the multitude, not the Just), an opportunity for a new beginning to accomplish this task. Each lot will have one hundred years to overcome sin.

157. **Isaiah 65:20** *There shall be no more thence an infant of days, nor an old man that hath not filled his days: for <u>the child shall die an hundred years old</u>; but the sinner being an hundred years old shall be accursed.*

ANOTHER DAY

The eighth day was the day of circumcision, a day of "rolling away the flesh." As all flesh was destroyed during the flood and only eight righteous people were saved, so will it be in the new beginning. The Bible leaves clues to these hidden secrets everywhere. Consider the clues we can see through the window left open through which we can only glimpse into God's plan:

158. **2 Peter 3:8** *But, beloved, be not ignorant of this one thing, that one day is with the Lord as a thousand years, and a thousand years as one day.*

For the past six thousand years man has ruled in the governments of this earth: four thousand years from Adam to Christ, and two thousand years from Christ to this day. Soon, this world will enter into the next millennium (the next thousand years) in which Christ will rule with a rod of iron, with his Bride in perfect government and perfect judgement.

159. **Deuteronomy 5:12-14** *Keep the sabbath day to sanctify it, as the LORD thy God hath commanded thee. Six days thou shalt labour, and do all thy work: But the seventh day is the sabbath of the LORD thy God: in it thou shalt not do any work, thou, nor thy son, nor thy daughter, nor thy manservant, nor thy maidservant, nor thine ox, nor thine ass, nor any of thy cattle, nor thy stranger that is within thy gates; that thy manservant and thy maidservant may rest as well as thou.*

160. **Hebrews 4:8-9** *For if Jesus had given them rest, then would he not afterward have spoken of another day. There remaineth therefore a rest to the people of God.*

After the seventh day (seventh thousand year period) is finished, the rest of the dead will live again. This will be the beginning of the first lot of the second resurrection. It will be known as the eighth day, the day of "cutting off of the flesh." People will have to sever sin from their life or be severed from life itself, and be cast into the judgement of the second death. (see Joshua 5:5-9).

Satan will be around to deceive these people (Revelation 20:3, 7-8), but the saints of God will be there, in that perfect day, to help. Also, there will be another advantage for them in relation to this government; that Righteousness will reign!

161. **2 Peter 3:13-14** *Nevertheless we, according to his promise, look for new heavens and a new earth, wherein dwelleth righteousness. Wherefore, beloved, seeing that ye look for such things, be diligent that ye may be found of him in peace, without spot, and blameless.*

162. **Isaiah 35:8** *And an highway shall be there, and a way, and it shall be called The way of holiness; the unclean shall not pass over it; but it shall be for those: the wayfaring men, though fools, shall not err therein.*

Even a fool could not mess up when righteousness reigns. They would have to intentionally refuse to perfect themselves. That highway, by definition as a winding staircase, signifies that each step higher is progressively rises towards perfection. Those that perfect themselves will be raised unto everlasting life. Those that do not will go down in the pages of history along with Satan. They will have been raised only to fail, with themselves only to blame. They will be merely a memory of everlasting shame and contempt.

163. **Daniel 12:2** *And many of them that sleep in the dust of the earth shall awake, some to everlasting life, and some to shame and everlasting contempt.*

164. **John 5:28-29** *Marvel not at this: for the hour is coming, in the which all that are in the graves shall hear his voice, And shall come forth; they that have done good, unto the resurrection of life; and they that have done evil, unto the resurrection of damnation.*

The translators used a harsh word when they interpreted the above passage as a resurrection of "damnation." A better translation would have been "judgment." Those that work sin out of their lives will be raised unto life everlasting. Those that don't get sin out of their lives will be raised unto a resurrection of judgement. Judgement still hangs over their heads, which could lead to damnation. They will be no more, exposed to God's judgement: "the lake of fire," to be spoken out of existence.

Work out your salvation with fear and trembling. Sin will be done away with, one way or another. God's Spirit will not always strive with men. Yet above all, He does! He has done, and will do all He can to help. Will He <u>not</u> finish what He has begun in you, with you, even unto this day? In learning these things, does He not care for you? He is the God of <u>love</u>. He promised that sin will be done away with for <u>our</u> sakes!

165. **Job 28:28** *And unto man he said, Behold, the fear of the Lord, that is wisdom; and to depart from evil is understanding.*

166. **Proverbs 3:19** *The LORD by wisdom hath founded the earth; by understanding hath he established the heavens.*

167. **Ezekiel 33:11-12** *Say unto them, As I live, saith the Lord GOD, I have no pleasure in the death of the wicked; but that the wicked turn from his way and live: turn ye, turn ye from your evil ways; for why will ye die, O house of Israel? Therefore, thou son of man, say unto the children of thy people, The righteousness of the righteous shall not deliver him in the day of his transgression: as for the wickedness of the wicked, he shall not fall thereby in the day that he turneth from his wickedness; neither shall the righteous be able to live for his righteousness in the day that he sinneth.*

Hell, temporary or permanent (chastisement or death consecutively) is God's punishment upon the disobedient, whether it is a person, or an entire nation. A condition of hell on earth is soon to come because of global rejection of Christ. They will not be cast in hell, but the world will be <u>turned into hell</u> (see #57).

168. **Psalms 9:17** *The wicked shall be turned into hell, and all the nations that forget God.*

To be "cast into hell" means to put, deposited, thrown with force, flung, or hurled. To be "turned into hell" is like the water that was turned into wine. Jesus did not hurl or cast wine into the water. The contents, water, were changed. The nations that forget God are not removed from their physical location into a physical place called hell. Instead, their joy is turned into sorrow, their laughter into weeping, and their prosperity into poverty. When they need help, God will forget them for forgetting Him. Life on Earth will become a living hell!

Criminals, denied a burial were thrown (cast) into the fires of the trash heap known as Gehenna. There was so much trash and corruption within it that the fire never went out. Beneath the burning trash was smothered material in which the flies continually laid their eggs (maggots). The steady reproduction, which fed on the corruption, turned it into worse corruption. This was what Jesus referred to as the worm that dieth not (Mark 9:44-48). The disobedient are never raised from corruption. Their decaying flesh has no hope of getting better, but only worse; being exposed to the worm that dieth not. Everlasting shame and contempt is what has happened to the names of Satan, or Hitler, etc. Their names go down in infamy!

169. **Isaiah 10:4** *Without me they shall bow down under the prisoners, and they shall fall under the slain. For all this his anger is not turned away, but his hand is stretched out still.*

170. **Proverbs 1:24-26** *Because I have called, and ye refused; I have stretched out my hand, and no man regarded... I also will laugh at your calamity; I will mock when your fear cometh;*

God stretched out his hands for us as a parent does for their children through His Son, Jesus Christ, on the cross. He still does so in many ways, every day. He has no pleasure in the death of the wicked. I sense His urgency in His words to every generation throughout the scriptures, especially as these days come to a close. I can feel His pain as He pleads with tears for all to choose life. Time is running out and hell is beginning to yawn for more souls. Satan's lies must be cut asunder with the Sword of Truth. Will you help put him to shame by joining in the chorus that he is a liar; that God is a God of love, not hate and evil vengeance, while you strive for perfection? Sing the song that no man can learn but the 144,000 (Revelation 14:3), which is the song of Moses and the song of the Lamb; Old & New Testament truth harmonized! (see Revelation 15:3). God takes sin seriously. Will you?

We should all be aware that Paul's battle against sin was just as serious as the battle against false doctrine.

171. **Isaiah 3:12** *As for my people, children are their oppressors, and women rule over them. O my people, they which lead thee cause thee to err, and destroy the way of thy paths.*

172. **2 Timothy 2:25-26** *In meekness instructing those that oppose themselves; if God peradventure will give them repentance to the acknowledging of the truth; And that they may recover themselves out of the snare of the devil, who are taken captive by him at his will.*

of heaven saying, ... the tabernacle of God ....n, and he will dwell wi.. .... ..d they shall be his people, ...d God himself shall be with them, and be their God.

4 And *f*God shall wipe away all tears from their eyes; and *g*there shall be no more death, *h*neither sorrow, nor crying, neither shall there be any more pain: for the former things are passed away.

5 And *i*he that sat upon the throne said, Behold, *j*I make all things new. And he said unto me, Write: for these words are

f Is. 25:8

g 1 Cor. 15:26, 54

h Is. 35:10
Is. 61:3

i ch. 4:2

j Is. 43:19
2 Cor. 5:17

k Is. 12:3
Is. 55:1
John 4:10, 14
John 7:37

l Rom. 8:17, 32

m Zech. 8:8
Heb. 8:10

n 1 Cor. 6:9
Gal. 5:19